THE
PLEASURES
OF LOVING GOD

MIKE BICKLE

CHARISMA
HOUSE

THE PLEASURES OF LOVING GOD by Mike Bickle
Published by Charisma House
Charisma Media/Charisma House Book Group
600 Rinehart Road
Lake Mary, Florida 32746
www.charismahouse.com

Unless otherwise noted, all Scripture quotations are from the New King James Version of the Bible. Copyright © 1979, 1980, 1982 by Thomas Nelson, Inc., publishers. Used by permission.

Scripture quotations marked KJV are from the King James Version of the Bible.

Scripture quotations marked NAS are from the New American Standard Bible. Copyright © 1960, 1962, 1963, 1968, 1971, 1972, 1973. 1975, 1977 by the Lockman Foundation. Used by permission. (www.Lockman.org)

Scripture quotations marked NIV are from the Holy Bible, New International Version. Copyright © 1973, 1978, 1984, International Bible Society. Used by permission.

Library of Congress Catalog Card Number: 00-108365
ISBN-13: 978-0-88419-662-4
E-Book ISBN: 978-1-59979-641-3

11 12 13 14 15 — 15 14 13 12 11
Printed in the United States of America

DEDICATION

I want to dedicate this book to my dear son, Luke, and his wonderful wife, Ricci, who are currently on the mission field in Mexico. May they experience the pleasures of loving God as they serve the orphans in Mexico. I thank Luke for his tireless zeal to help lead the prayer meetings (midnight to 6:00 A.M.) each night in the early months of birthing the International House of Prayer in Kansas City. I remember the times I came there in the middle of the night without Luke knowing. Hiding in a back room, I so enjoyed listening through the walls to Luke crying out to God for revival in the nations. What a joy that was to my heart. Proverbs 10:1 says, "A wise son makes a glad father." Thank you, Luke, for making my heart glad as I enjoy your devotion to Jesus and your dedication to the House of Prayer. Thank you, Ricci, for being the genuine woman of God that you are.

ACKNOWLEDGMENTS

I appreciate Amelia Fuller for the countless hours of her time and for her energy that she freely dedicated to transcribe the sermons from which this book was developed. I am inspired by her tears in the prayer rooms and her labor at the computer. Thank you, Deborah Perkins, for the hours you spent merging and editing transcriptions. Your devotion to Jesus is remarkable, and your genuine desire to serve in a secret place is rare and inspiring. I am grateful to Renee DeLoriea for working with skill and spiritual depth to turn the transcripts into a real book. Renee, you were a joy to work with. It is refreshing to see professional abilities used by the Holy Spirit in the way that yours are. Peg deAlminana's insightful and skillful editing was invaluable. You were brilliant. Thank you.

Contents

International House of Prayer

On September 19, 1999, we began a twenty-four-a-day intercessory worship ministry in Kansas City. We are training singers, musicians and intercessors to flow in the prophetic anointing in an interactive way. Ideally, we have between ten and fifteen singers on each worship team. Central to our model is praying (singing) the Scriptures, using the New Testament apostolic prayers, the hymns of Revelation, the Psalms and the Song of Solomon.

We have three types of prayer meetings:

- Intercessory worship in which we engage in spiritual warfare for revival

- Devotional prayer meetings that provide an anointed atmosphere to sit at the feet of Jesus

- "Worship from the Word" meetings, which are comprised of singing the Psalms, the Song of Solomon and the hymns of Revelation in a corporate antiphonal way. We are in the early development of antiphonal choirs.

Our vision is to train and send out teams to plant Houses of Prayer throughout the earth. Currently we have approximately one hundred people who have raised their own support as "intercessory missionaries." Another one hundred fifty are in the process of relocating to Kansas City for training. We also have groups of visitors that come and usually stay up to a week in accommodations that we make available at very low costs. Throughout the week we conduct "One-Day Seminars" designed to train our visitors.

For more information about our present structure, principles, One-Day Seminars, training programs, short-term housing or ministry resources, visit our website at www.ihopkc.com.

FOREWORD

My FRIEND MIKE Bickle really is a God chaser—and his life proves it! That's why the message of this book will resonate in the hearts of God chasers everywhere.

When a father holds and plays with his children, who derives pleasure from the encounter? The children think that they do, but the dad knows that he does! So it is with God. God enjoys the encounter of our worship, and we receive the pleasure of His presence in return. In this powerful book, Mike Bickle illustrates the truth of that principle and shows us how to rekindle passionate love for God and rediscover His pleasure at our presence.

In *The Pleasures of Loving God,* Mike Bickle shares his heart in an open, refreshing way. He reveals how, as the son of a tough boxer, his own identity was redefined as a lover of God. He learned that God enjoys being with him—and he wants you to know that God enjoys being with you, too!

Whether plunging to the depths of divine intimacy or the

heights of holy passion, this book often echoes my own ponderings. In my recent writings, it occurred to me that when passion is restored, the joy of "presence" returns. Now I am freshly reminded by Mike Bickle that "at [His] right hand are pleasures forevermore" (Ps. 16:11).

If you want to raise the spiritual temperature of your heart, if you want to hasten the pace of your chase, if your soul is thirsty and longs to know God more, then this book is for you. Thank you, Mike, for reminding us of *The Pleasures of Loving God.*

—TOMMY TENNEY

AUTHOR OF NUMEROUS BEST-SELLING BOOKS, INCLUDING

THE GOD CHASERS AND *GOD'S SECRET TO GREATNESS*

Introduction

O N OCCASION PEOPLE have asked me the question, "What is the key to living a happy life?"

I tell them what I believe to be "the secret" to happiness and enjoying life. Actually, it is not a secret at all. The truth is that those who live for Jesus can enjoy life when we begin to see that God actually likes us! That God enjoys and likes us even in our weakness is an idea that some find difficult to accept.

I am really beginning to believe that I am one of God's favorites! Now, that may sound arrogant to you until you understand that God has millions of favorites. Through the lens of the passion of His own heart and the gift of righteousness, God sees us as those He loves even as He loves His own Son. (See John 15:9; 17:23.) This fact makes us God's favorites. As I grow in my understanding as one of God's favorite people, and as I grasp the living reality that He really likes me, then I have a key foundational reality that helps me to enjoy life.

The essence of this book is a challenge for the bride of

Christ, the church, to mature in voluntary love for Jesus and thus for one another. The Father wants a bride for His Son whose love will endure in times of testing.

One of my favorite books in the Bible is the Song of Solomon. My testimony is that of being a spiritually dull man whom God has empowered to love Him. Yes, I love Him imperfectly, but I love Him more than I ever imagined possible in my earlier days. I know much about struggle and failure. But I also know about being embraced by God's tenderness and mercy.

When you are in love, it's much easier to do things for the one you love. Spending time with Jesus isn't a big sacrifice when we feel the power of love flowing through us. In fact, it isn't a sacrifice at all because it's something we want to do.

My current ministry enables me to spend much time with the Lord on a regular basis. By the grace of God, we have established a twenty-four-hour House of Prayer in Kansas City, and now it is my job to spend long hours worshiping the Lord!

The Lord released us to worship Him for twenty-four hours a day in September 1999. Though we have just begun to build this House of Prayer, the Lord is giving us fresh strategies to fulfill His purposes by worshiping Him and thus releasing Holy Spirit activity into the earth.

Currently, an army of intercessors committed to living a fasted lifestyle is coming forth. Their source of strength and joy comes from enjoying intimacy with God and thereby reaping the benefits of having deeply personal moments with Him. Intercessors have often seen themselves as being on the shelf serving in back rooms in the church. The time has come for them to begin to emerge as an integral part of the working body of Christ that will be fulfilling the Great Commission out of hearts of love for Jesus, rather than from a sense of duty.

Have you been laboring to a point of exhaustion and

discouragement? Do you find yourself constantly repenting from one type of failure, only to find that another pops up to take its place? Laboring to fulfill the Great Commission solely out of a sense of duty can lead to burnout. That's because God never designed the human race to work first and love second. If our priorities are out of order, and our main focus is on the work, burnout may be somewhere around the corner. You were simply not designed to put love on the back burner. It must be front and center in our lives.

This book is an adventure in enjoying our relationship with Jesus. I hope it will help some to see more clearly why it is important and how it can be done. This love relationship with the Godhead is so important as we move closer to the end of the age. Worshiping Him under the canopy of His love will provide safety, protection and provision even during times of great judgment on the earth.

God the Father wants a lovesick bride for His Son, Jesus. He wants a church that loves everything about Jesus, not one that picks and chooses what characteristics of Christ meet its fancy and which ones do not. We must love all of Him, His mercy as well as His judgments.

In essence, that is the summation of this book. It is a challenge for the bride of Christ to love Jesus with mature love. The Father wants a bride for His Son whose love will endure in times of testing.

You know, being beaten up and beaten down really isn't a key component for being holy. True holiness can only come through a love relationship with the God we enjoy. I call it happy holiness. Harsh threats will only have temporary effects. God the Father doesn't want a bride for His Son who has been threatened into submission. For His Son, He wants a pure love, a willing heart—a bride who is a lover and not just a servant.

Knowing that the Lord deeply enjoys you right now, at this very moment, will change your life. It's invigorating! Yes, you can take a deep breath, rest and be excited about the fact that God doesn't see us the way many of us see ourselves. He does not define us by our struggles, but rather He defines us by His passion for us and our longing to be a lover of God.

He sees you as He designed you to be: a lover of His Son, Jesus. Satan, as the accuser of the brethren, wants to define your life according to your struggles and failures. Why? So that you will live demoralized in condemnation and a sense of spiritual defeat and hopelessness.

Your life will experience some significant changes when you realize that the Lord enjoys the very thought of you. You make God smile. Once you realize how much the Lord really likes you, loving Him will just naturally follow.

As you read this book, ask the Holy Spirit to help you discover that you are, indeed, God's favorite.

AT YOUR RIGHT HAND ARE PLEASURES FOREVERMORE.

—PSALM 16:11

1

YOUR IDENTITY
AS A LOVER

DURING THE LAST ten years, I have had the opportunity to interact with several men with powerful anointings and a wide platform of ministry. The Lord has used them mightily to release His supernatural power. So I was quite surprised when these spiritual giants confided to me how they were bored even while leading large and dynamic ministries—and even felt bored with being used in the power of God.

For example, I was doing a large conference in Europe with a well-known man of God, and I witnessed powerful demonstrations of the Holy Spirit. After the meeting, I could hardly wait to ask him what he had felt when, during the service, a lady screamed out in joy after being instantly healed. I was very surprised at his answer.

He said, "I was glad for her, but personally I have grown accustomed to such demonstrations." Then he continued, "I still feel the same way in my lonely hotel room after the meeting—bored." He went on to describe his bitterness from various disappointments that had a hold of him.

I remember thinking, *Surely doing miracles in Jesus' name would cause life to be filled with excitement.* I blurted out those words, and he responded, "At first that's how we all feel. But over time we are confronted with our own spiritual bankruptcy if we do not encounter God in a deep and continual way."

This man is not the only minister of the gospel who ended up feeling bored with it all. Many have quietly expressed their dissatisfaction. Experiencing years of God using their hands to heal the sick, using their words to inspire and change lives and using their dreams and visions to reach beyond the natural realm only left them dissatisfied in their spirits. Many mighty generals of the church end up not enjoying God and struggling to find intimacy with Him. Yet, despite their personal spiritual dryness, their ministries continued to flourish.

At one time, I thought that being anointed in ministry would keep a person's heart encouraged in God. Now I've learned this is simply not true! A deeply satisfied soul, a personal sense of meaning and significance and a rich treasure store of divine pleasure can only come through the intimate knowledge of God Himself.

Do you seek spiritual renewal? Do you desire divine satisfaction beyond your greatest imaginations? Then focus on two things: First, focus on the intimate knowledge of God's beauty, or what God looks like (in terms of knowing His personality). Second, focus on the knowledge of what it means to be created in His image, in other words, what we look like to God in Christ. These two arenas of truth will invigorate your heart like nothing else. In this chapter, we will explore the importance of knowing who He is (what He looks like) and who we are in Him (what we look like to God). If we are to truly enjoy the Lord—or be renewed—we must also understand our true identity as new creatures in Christ Jesus.

The truth of our beauty being imparted to us by the beautiful God is a subject that will fascinate and exhilarate our hearts throughout all eternity. Imagine, the beauty Jesus possesses is the very beauty that He imparts to His bride in the gift of righteousness.

In recent years, discussion of renewal and revival has flourished. In this book, I will seek to show that long-lasting personal renewal comes primarily through the revelatory knowledge that I am desired and pursued by God and that I am fascinated by who He is. In response to that knowledge, I become a wholehearted lover of God. When my identity rests in the fact that I am loved by the beautiful God and therefore, I am a lover of God, then I am happy in my relationship with Him.

This reality awakens a profoundly deep sense of security and contentment—to know that we are living, not only as people loved by Him, but as those who are wholehearted in response. I must *know* I am wholehearted with God. Many see themselves as halfhearted hypocrites. This very accusation against their sincerity in God shuts down their hearts in a substantial way.

The glory of knowing I am pursued by a God who deeply desires me, even in my weakness, is awesome knowledge. Our emotional chemistry cannot but help be changed in the wake of this stunning reality.

Through this revelation, we find freedom from striving to attain a certain spiritual level to convince God to love and enjoy us. We can truly and deeply know that God passionately enjoys us. He adores and desires us, even as we struggle to

3

mature and grow in Him.

Because I am enjoying God, I sin less, quit less and divide less in respect to my relationships with my brothers and sisters in Christ. When I enjoy the Lord, I obey more, serve Him with greater perseverance and endure hardships with greater patience. In other words, I am renewed in my spirit and in my spiritual identity. Things that were once difficult for me now flow freely.

Feeling enjoyed by God releases even more grace to persevere in obedience, service and hardships. As this reality increases in me, I serve the Lord with joy, and I learn to enjoy Him.

Such are the confessions of believers who are happy in the Lord because we know that the Lord desires us—therefore, we are lovers of God. In fact, renewal is simply being happy in the Lord.

RESONATING WITH GOD

A TUNING FORK is an instrument with two long metal prongs that create a constant pitch. You've probably seen one at some time in your life. Strike the fork, and sound is created as the vibrations of one of the prongs causes the other prong to resonate with it. The energy of one prong is sustained by its proximity to the energy of the other prong.

We were created by God to resonate with Him. We come alive and are invigorated when we come in contact with the fascinating knowledge of the uncreated God who enjoys us, desires us and has redeemed us.

We can draw a very important principle about personal renewal from Colossians 3:10: "And have put on the new man who is renewed in knowledge according to the image of Him who created him." In this passage, Paul outlines two arenas of knowledge. The first is the knowledge according to the image of God. Another word for image here could be the word *personality.* The first thing Paul learned before the Lord was that the knowledge of the personality of God encourages obedience; it motivates people to repent and encourages their hearts.

This portion of Scripture is key to our quest to walk in repentance and personal renewal. Nothing can come close to awakening and encouraging the heart as can the marvelous knowledge of the image of God—there is simply nothing more renewing than this!

This is key to your own personal renewal and to ushering others into wholehearted commitment to the Lord as well. The knowledge of the personality of God, the knowledge of what God is like, will win your friends and loved ones to the Lord. A genuine understanding of the knowledge of the personality of God is probably the area in which the church is most lacking.

Something awakens inside of us when we know what God is like. He designed us so that our spirits will dull when we have a void of the knowledge of God's beauty. Our spirits will become progressively more dull and callous if we are not coming into regular, fresh contact with the Word of God where the Holy Spirit reveals to us what God is like.

The prophet Isaiah said that we would call the Messiah "Wonderful" (Isa. 9:6). He is the One who would fill the church with wonderment. Oh, the power of living in the power of endless wonder! We were made to marvel and be stunned. We live bored when wonderment is gone. He will be called *the Wonderful God.*

The knowledge of God is what makes sin look foolish and

righteousness look excellent. It makes persevering in hardships seem reasonable, and it produces in our spirits a big "Yes!" response to obeying a call to the will of God. This knowledge will awaken the hearts of God's people—and the hearts of unbelievers.

Satan and his host of demons work hard to blind our minds from understanding the glory and person of God. (See 2 Corinthians 4:4.) The devil knows that if he can blind our understanding to what God is like, he has then leveraged the battle significantly in his favor. He accuses God in our hearts. He seeks to fill the church with lies that rise up to accuse the truth of God in our hearts. When this occurs, spiritual boredom results. A spiritually bored believer is more vulnerable to Satan's attacks.

A vital aspect of personal renewal is *repentance*. Alongside of using the phrase "coming into a deeper state of repentance," we may actually speak of "being motivated by enjoying the Lord" or "being glad in the Lord."

Let's further examine Colossians 3:10:

> And have put on the new man who is renewed in knowledge according to the image of Him who created him.

Most Bible translations link the image of God to the image of believers who are created anew in Christ Jesus.

> Put on the new man, which after God is created in righteousness and true holiness.
>
> —EPHESIANS 4:24

Ephesians 4:24, which is the companion verse of Colossians 3:10, makes it clear that Paul is referring to the believer who is made new in Christ Jesus. In Colossians 3:10, Paul is referring to

6

our spiritual identity in Christ Jesus, not to our natural identity.

I do not claim to have the greatest of experiences in all of this. But I do claim to understand a little bit about how to enjoy the Lord. My own experience and my study of the Word of God, church history and the testimonies of great men and women of God have convinced me that there is nothing that awakens our hearts to wholehearted love like the times when God reveals Himself to us through His written Word. Nothing awakens our hearts with motivation, joy and pleasure like having the Holy Spirit as our escort, so to speak, put His arm around us and walk us into that divine treasury where God reveals Himself to us.

RENEWAL AND THE WORD

IF WE EXAMINE the Scriptures, it becomes clear that there is a very distinct biblical methodology to renewal, or to repentance—a sub-department of renewal. In His Word, God has revealed a strategy that renews us and renews the people we want to touch. That renewal is most effectively accomplished when we bring ourselves or others into contact with the following:

- The knowledge of the image of God

- The knowledge of the image of our spiritual identity in Christ (knowing who we are in Christ)

There are other things in the kingdom of God that contribute to renewal. But Colossians 3:10 and Ephesians 4:24 demonstrate that these two aspects of spiritual knowledge bring our hearts into renewal more than anything else.

Most of us usually try to encourage people in ways that do

not pertain to these two primary renewing truths. We mistakenly believe that if we only affirm people, we will thereby renew them. However, affirmation alone will not have long-term effects. Yes, I do believe in affirmation. I do believe in taking people out to dinner, telling them how important they are to us and spending time with them. I do think it is very important to do these kinds of things. But this kind of support will not renew people as will the revelation knowledge of the two truths described above. An individual's greater need will always be to be renewed in the knowledge of the image of God and the knowledge of the image of who he or she is in Christ Jesus.

I am not saying that developing relationships with people and affirming them is not important. We may have numerous ways to encourage people, but typically those ways are not related to Colossians 3:10. So it is not surprising that typically our renewal efforts over the long haul have been fairly ineffective.

Therefore, it is very important for pastors to bring believers into systematic, regular contact with what the Word of God says about the knowledge of God and the knowledge of who they are in God. It is important for outreach efforts to be bathed in communications that reflect these two primary premises to bring long-lasting renewal. Getting a grip on who He is and who we are in Him will also revolutionize how we relate to one another. It literally changes our emotional chemistry to encounter the majesty, beauty, sweet affection, stunning mystery and splendor of our beloved God, Jesus Christ.

Reaching a place of spiritual lethargy is common during the course of months and years of serving God. I have slipped into this on several occasions over the years, and I never seem to be aware of it until I get through it. Sometimes I find myself in dry times when I am more spiritually passive than in other seasons. From the Word of God, I know that the way to remedy the problem in my spirit is described in Colossians 3:10. Here the remedy is spelled out very clearly. When my heart feels dull and lethargic, I try to bring myself into contact with these two dynamic truths outlined there: the knowledge of God and the knowledge of the image of my spiritual destiny in Christ.

I have found that people who are depressed usually do not know who the Lord is concerning them and who they are before the Lord.

LIVING FROM YOUR SPIRITUAL IDENTITY

BECAUSE IT IS very easy to do so, most of us live through our emotions, which are based on our natural identities. When we live out of our natural identities, we define ourselves by how much money we make, what position and abilities we possess, how much power and influence we have and who we know. The Lord, on the other hand, wants us to live out of the resources and the power of our spiritual identity—in other words, defining our lives by the fact that the beautiful God desires us and has exalted us in the gift of the righteousness of Jesus. Moving away from relying on our natural identity to a place where we live our lives out of our spiritual identity will keep us in a constant state of renewal. It will invigorate and encourage our hearts like nothing else.

In my own personal life, I realized that having a growing ministry still did not satisfy my need for significance and excitement. It was in the summer of 1990. My conference ministry had grown internationally in a sudden way, and my ministry had experienced financial prosperity and increase that year far beyond anything I had ever anticipated. About three thousand people attended my local church, and over eight thousand people attended our annual church conference that summer in Kansas City.

But when all the crowds were gone, and it was just me and my weary body lying in bed, I felt the same dissatisfied feeling that I had grown so accustomed to in earlier years. I had always thought that growth in ministry would take care of that sense of inner emptiness. But I had to face the fact that I was wrong.

That was the summer that God began to open the Song of Solomon to me in a deeply personal way. The Lord unfolded the truths of this book to me over several weeks. The passage in Song of Solomon 7:10, "I am my beloved's, and his desire is toward me," had an unusual personal application to my heart. I felt wooed into a vast ocean of God's burning desire for me. I felt profoundly satisfied as the object of His burning desire. I remember crying out to God, "If I never speak again on a platform, I feel crowned with honor and glory in Your love." I began to discover my spiritual identity.

DISCOVERING YOUR SPIRITUAL IDENTITY

HOW THE LORD established and revealed to Simon Peter his spiritual identity begins to unfold in a wonderful way in John 13. Simon Peter, the chief apostle among the twelve, would later deny the Lord three times on the night that Jesus was betrayed. But in John 13:10, Jesus makes a very interesting statement; He tells the twelve disciples who are sitting around at the Last Supper, "And you are clean, though not every one of you" (NIV). He was referring to Judas when He said that there was one exception.

Jesus looked them right in the face and said that only one

of them was not clean, and that was because that one had a betraying heart.

I always thought of Peter before the Day of Pentecost as weak and immature in God. This was true, but it did not make him dirty. Jesus told these immature apostles that they were clean. What a perspective! How could they be immature spiritually without being dirty to God? Because spiritual immaturity is not the same as rebellion, which is the condition of those who are unclean before God.

We find additional information about the event in Matthew. Jesus said:

> All of you will be made to stumble because of Me this night, for it is written: "I will strike the Shepherd, and the sheep of the flock will scattered."
> —MATTHEW 26:31

Then in verses 33–34:

> Peter answered and said to Him, "Even if all are made to stumble because of You, I will never be made to stumble."
> Jesus said to him, "Assuredly, I say to you that this night, before the rooster crows, you will deny Me three times."

When the Lord tells Peter that the rooster is going to crow, He created a prophetic parable of Peter's spiritual pride. Peter validated the analogy when he said, "Even if I have to die with You, I will not deny You!" (v. 35).

Jesus had said, "Everyone of you will stumble." But during that very same conversation in John 13:10, He also told them, "All of you are clean."

How could they be sure to stumble and still be clean? It's because there is a great difference between stumbling in the

11

weakness of our flesh and having a betraying heart that is in rebellion against God. In God's eyes, it is not contradictory to call the group clean in John 13:10, while at the same time telling them in Matthew 26:31 they would all stumble in immaturity.

Do you know that you can stumble without falling? Do you know that you can come up short and still be clean before the Lord? This does not mean that your sin does not matter. But it is extremely important to remember that God still sees the cry of your heart. Even when you stumble, He still recognizes that you have a willing spirit—that you still have genuine love for Him. We are not hopeless hypocrites when we stumble. Satan wants to convince us that we are not genuine lovers of God because we are weak in our flesh, but there is a vast difference between spiritual immaturity and rebellion. To confuse these two is to position ourselves for severe spiritual setbacks.

Do not misunderstand, God's affection for us in our weakness is not the same as His agreement or approval of the area of our lives in which we sin. He disciplines us because He disagrees with sin. However, it is precisely because of His affection for us that He does discipline us. He does not discipline us because He is writing us off, rather because He wants intimacy with us.

He is not passive about sin in our lives when we fall short of His command, even though we have a willing spirit. However, He is not exasperated with us. He longs to have deep intimacy with us. But there is something that is even beyond tripping and stumbling in our well-intentioned efforts to walk in faith.

In Luke 22:32 we find added information about this conversation. Jesus says to Peter:

> But I have prayed for you, that your faith should not fail; and
> when you have returned to Me, strengthen your brethren.

Essentially, the Lord tells Simon that He is going to pray for him, so that although he would betray the Lord, Simon Peter would not fall.

You may be scratching your head and saying, "Now wait a minute! If you stumble, doesn't that indicate that you have fallen and that your faith has failed?"

Actually, there is a difference between a believer with a sincere heart who encounters the weakness of his flesh and a person with a betraying heart against God who goes beyond stumbling and actually falls in his faith. There is a state of having a betraying heart.

The Lord's language distinguishes between these two categories. Looking at the difference between these two heart conditions is extremely important, because when we stumble and come up short, we often make the mistake of labeling ourselves as rebels.

Nevertheless, there is a vast difference between immaturity and rebellion. The immature believer is the one who is immature in the faith. There may be a few exceptions, but most of us are still very immature in our faith when compared to someone like the apostle Paul. The immature believer, someone who is still immature in his faith, will stumble. He may even say things and do things that are incongruent with walking in obedience to the Lord.

Following this discussion at the Last Supper, they went to the Garden of Gethsemane. Here Jesus revisits this discussion. In Matthew 26:41, Jesus looks at Peter and describes his heart to him in two ways. Jesus told Peter that he had a willing spirit and weak flesh—both at the same time.

> Watch and pray, lest you enter into temptation. The spirit
> indeed is willing, but the flesh is weak.

Although the New International Version translates the
word *flesh* as "body," I don't believe that Christ is talking
about the physical body here. I believe Jesus is speaking
about the principle of the flesh, that propensity to yield to
sin under pressure.

Jesus understood the apparent contradiction in Peter
because He understood the frame of man. Psalm 103:14 tells
us that God remembers that we are but dust.

> For He knows our frame; He remembers that we are
> dust.

Peter's problem was that he did not realize his flesh was
weak. He genuinely believed that he was never going to deny
the Lord. He thought that he would never come up short.
Peter, in his immaturity, had more confidence in his own commitment to the Lord than in the Lord's commitment to him.

This misconception is where most believers begin. In fact,
it's where I began. When I met the Lord, I was so excited. In
fact, I think I was probably more excited about me than I was
about the Lord. I thought the Lord had gotten the deal of the
century—me!

I was just like Peter. My attitude was, "I won't stumble.
Lord, don't worry about me. Go take care of those other
guys. I'll be there for You all the time!"

I could have put my name right in that passage of Peter's
and taken it personally! It could have looked something like
this: The Lord would say, "OK, Mike, you are going to stumble
because you have weak flesh. But, you do have a willing spirit."

Then I would have said, "Not me, Lord. I am not going to

stumble! Those other guys will stumble." Because I didn't understand my weakness in those early years, I thought that the Lord had really gotten Himself a good deal. Later, I remember how confused I became as the Lord opened my eyes to see the weakness of my own flesh.

It is hard for many of us to grasp the fact that God loves us and enjoys us—even in our immaturity. We are lovers of God even in immaturity. When we stumble, we often see ourselves as hopeless hypocrites, and we lose the confession within our own souls that we are lovers of God. We listen to an accusing spirit instead of holding fast to the truth about who God says we are in Christ Jesus. We begin to believe the lies of the enemy that accuse us, telling us that we are hopeless hypocrites who do not really love God.

When Peter stumbled, he was still a lover of God. Because of the work of Christ, he was still clean before God.

I Am Loved, and I Am a Lover

I CAN BE confident in the fact that God loves me in my immaturity, and in my immaturity, I return my love back to Him. Along with that, because I am loved and I am a lover, I am successful in my humanity as a person during my time on the earth. My primary success is because of that one spiritual principle and fact: I am loved, and I am a lover of God. No matter what else happens, in the most profound way, I am already successful because I have received His free love and have become a follower of Jesus.

Even though Peter stumbles and denies his Lord in Matthew 26, the Lord goes after him and meets him in John 21. In this passage, the resurrected Jesus encounters Peter face to face for the first time following Peter's denial.

In John 21:15-17, the Lord comes to Peter to help him recover his faith. At this point Peter, no doubt, felt like a hopeless hypocrite, having just denied the Lord after he had sworn that it was the one thing he would never do. Scripture suggests that Peter had given up on the idea of being an apostle. In his heart, Peter was probably saying, "I love You, God, but I know that I'm disqualified. I know that I can't stand before You as I did before. I'm just too big a failure!"

In this passage of Scripture, the Lord asks him the same question three times: "Simon, son of Jonah, do you love me?"

Jesus was asking Peter a very important question. He did not ask Peter this question because He needed the information. Jesus asked this question because Peter, shaken to the very core by his own failure, desperately needed the information about himself.

Just eight days prior, when Jesus and Peter were in the Garden of Gethsemane, the Lord had told Peter that his flesh was weak. I can imagine their conversation going something like this: The Lord said to Peter, "I told you something else about your heart, Peter, which you didn't understand. I told you that you had a willing spirit. Peter, when I look at you, I see a 'Yes' in your spirit. You have a willing spirit. You have a 'Yes' in your spirit to Me. You are actually a genuine lover of God before Me, Peter. So I want to ask you, do you love Me?"

I imagine Peter saying something like, "Yeah, I guess, in the light of that I do. You really . . . "

The Lord then might have interrupted, "Yes, Peter, you are a lover of God. You are not a hopeless hypocrite. You're not disqualified, Peter. You've discovered the weakness of your flesh. I couldn't trust you until you saw it."

The criterion or basis of ministry in Peter's mind was his

16

strength and ability to serve God. But the criterion of ministry in Christ's mind was completely different. It was love. Peter's genuine love for Jesus qualified him to serve as an apostle, not Peter's ability to never stumble. As I stated earlier, Peter at first had more confidence in his commitment to Jesus than in Jesus' commitment to him. Peter's security in God was based on his own ability never to fall. But after this difficult time, Peter's security was in the fact that he was loved by God.

In asking the question three times, Christ was reestablishing new criteria from which Peter's ministry would be launched in the future.

UNDERSTANDING YOUR WEAKNESS

MEN AND WOMEN in the kingdom of God who do not have a healthy revelation of the weakness of their own flesh are dangerous if God anoints them for leadership and ministry. They can wreak havoc in the kingdom of God through spiritual pride.

There is nothing more abusive than a leader anointed in ministry who does not have a humble revelation of the weakness of his flesh. Self-righteousness, spiritual abuse and misuse of spiritual authority can all stem from this problem. A lot of crazy things happen outside the context of this twofold revelation. We are reckless with pride if we do not know that we have weak flesh. But when we see our weakness, we begin to despair if we do not know that we have a willing spirit. God wants neither reckless pride nor despairing condemnation. Rather, He wants us secure in love, secure that He enjoys us in love and that our love, though weak, is still seen as genuine by God.

Like Peter, we often get a revelation of the weakness of our flesh, but we lose the revelation that we have a willing spirit before God. We say, "Lord, we're committed! We'll never stumble!" Then two years later we are saying, "Lord, I am so weak—I'm a hopeless hypocrite!" If Satan cannot get us by reckless pride, then he will seek to destroy our confidence in love by making us feel condemned as hopeless hypocrites.

We must come to the realization of both of these aspects: We are weak in our flesh, and we have a willing spirit. Both are necessary for healthy spiritual growth.

THREE CONFESSIONS OF LOVE

IN JOHN 21:15, Peter says:

Yes, Lord; You know that I love You.

I see him kind of stumbling around, finally whispering a shame-filled answer: "You know that I'm a lover of God." In verse 16 Jesus again asks:

Simon, son of Jonah, do you love Me?

I can now imagine Peter saying, "Oh, this question hurts me! I hate this! I'm a hypocrite. I failed You! I denied You, God. I can't be a leader. I am disqualified permanently. There's no way..."

The Lord may have lifted Peter's chin, so as to look eye to eye, and then replied, "Peter, look at Me. Do you remember when we were in the garden? I told you that you had a willing spirit. I see in you a cry to be a lover of God, Peter. Yes, you have weak flesh, but you have a willing spirit. Do you remember? I said that you were clean, and at that very moment I told you that you would deny Me. You stumbled, but you have not fallen. You have now confronted your weakness, but your heart has betrayed Me. You are immature, but you are not rebellious, Peter."

In verse 16, I imagine the tone of that second reply as having more resolve. "You're … right … Lord. You know I … love … You."

In His heart, the Lord might have been thinking something like this: "Peter, you've denied Me three times, and I want to break the shame of those three denials over your life. That is why you must speak the truth—that you are a lover of God—three times."

Jesus was breaking the power of shame related to Peter's failure in order to reinstate him into a position of confidence in the throne of grace. This, however, is not the only thing happening in this passage.

So often when we fall and come up short, we want to shut out the grace of God. We want to put ourselves on probation or into purgatory for a season. We beat ourselves up emotionally for a while, thinking that by doing so we will somehow come to deserve forgiveness. But when we do, we are placing our confidence in something other than the burning love of Jesus and the finished work of the cross. If we fix our eyes and hearts on the finished work that was accomplished in His death, the Lord will then come to us and cause us to confess the truth of who we are before Him.

Jesus looks at Peter and asks him the same question for the third time. This time Peter replies:

> Lord, You know all things; You know that I love You.
>
> —JOHN 21:17

Many of us, in the midst of failure, cannot even make this

statement to the Lord because we don't believe it. Our hearts are locked tightly with shame. We would never dare imagine that the God who knows all things actually knows that we are genuine lovers of Jesus. Instead, we become so focused on our stumbling that we are washed away by despair, losing sight of the fact that we are lovers of God and are loved by God.

Peter has taken a journey. At the outset, he was primarily defined by his identity in his ability to be committed to God and in what he could accomplish for God. In his pride, he fell. He was then defined by his failure—he took on the identity of that failure when he saw his own weakness. He found his identity in his shame and failure.

But the Lord Himself reestablished Peter's torn-down identity. Afterward, Peter no longer defined himself through his sense of human power or failure, or even through what he believed others might think. The Lord came back in resurrected power, looked into Peter's face and gave him bold new definition: "You are loved, and you are a lover."

THE ONE GOD LOVES

THE APOSTLE JOHN responded differently than Peter did. John defined himself through the Lord's burning affection for him. He identified himself as the one Christ loves. This can be seen in this portion of Scripture:

> Then Peter, turning around, saw the disciple whom Jesus loved following, who also had leaned on His breast at the supper.
>
> —JOHN 21:20

This is the Gospel written personally by the apostle John,

and John is talking about himself in this verse. Instead of saying, "Peter and John said to the Lord, . . . " he says, "Peter and the one God loves." He does not call himself by his name.

John is basically saying, "I don't know about these other guys and why they wallow in their shame and failure. As for me, I know that I am the one God loves."

Throughout the Gospel of John, he refers to himself in this manner five times. Can you imagine writing about yourself five times in the Word of God and saying, "Sam and the one God loves went to the meeting," instead of "Sam and I went to the meeting"?

John is saying, "I failed just as Peter did." As you may recall, Matthew 26 describes how Jesus said that all of them would stumble. John, in turn, was saying, "I know I stumbled, but I'm the one God loves. I know God likes me."

I so enjoy using this verse in times of worship. I come before Jesus and describe myself as the one God likes. I say, "Jesus, here I am, the one You enjoy; it is me again—Your favorite one." In the righteousness of Christ, we all have the right to present ourselves to God as "His favorite one." Try it.

There is so much to this. John is to the New Testament what David is to the Old Testament. John had that unique revelation of God's pleasure in him, even in his weak humanity. Jesus Christ had established John's identity as a lover.

You are one of Christ's chosen, just as John and Peter were. Therefore, these disciples' confessions apply to you, too. There are two confessions presented in verses 17 and 20 of John 21. John's confession in verse 20 is that you are the disciple whom God likes. In addition, you are also the disciple whom the Lord sees as a genuine lover of God. This is the confession of Peter in verse 17 when he says, "You know that I love You."

This is the glorious twofold definition of your life before God. This is your identity as a new creation in Christ. You are the one God loves, and you are a genuine lover of God. Even when you are discovering the weakness of your own flesh, these two essential confessions best describe your spiritual identity.

John denied the Lord the same way Peter did that night. However, unlike so many of us, John did not plummet into an emotional pit of self-recrimination and self-abuse. He was aware that the Lord loved him even through his faults. Great power and freedom are found in refusing to listen to the enemy's accusations and remaining unmoved in your identity as a genuine lover of God.

Knowing who we are before the Lord begins by having the same confession as John, of knowing, "I'm the one God likes, even with all that sin. Yes, I'm the one God likes. Yes, I'm the one whom God enjoys." That is the first confession.

I like to say to the Lord, "I'm loved, and I'm a lover; therefore, I am successful." The entirety of this confession is important because this spiritual identity gives renewal. The first part of the confession, knowing who we are in the Lord, is just one part of renewal. The next step is to hold fast to the confession that says, "I'm a lover of God."

FINDING YOUR DEFINITION AS A LOVER

SOMETIMES MY MINISTRY has good cycles in which it goes well, and sometimes it has bad cycles when I cannot sense the anointing of God's presence and the people seem bored. Sometimes my circumstances have cycles of blessing, and sometimes I have life cycles where I can hardly see any blessing at all. Sometimes my health is very good, and sometimes it has been assaulted. Sometimes my most important relationships are healthy; sometimes they are being undermined. But none of these circumstances ever change the fact, the bedrock of truth, that I am loved and that I am a lover. In the most absolute sense, I am successful before God. When pressures come in all areas of life, the confession that brings me comfort, the confession that brings me out of despair, is this: I am loved. I am a lover. Therefore, I am successful.

It may have been more difficult for Peter to say those words than it was for John, but it no longer has to be difficult for you. You do not have to listen to the voice of the accuser that may come through your spouse, your children, your parents or your best friends. In fact, they may call you everything else. They may even define you by your weaknesses, flaws and failures, but remember, you are *not* defined by the areas with which you struggle. You are defined as one who loves God and one whom God loves. That is the essential definition of your life.

This powerful definition will bring forth lifelong repentance that grows stronger and mightier in the inner man. The knowledge of who He is and the knowledge of who we are in Him bring lasting renewal to our own spirits, affecting every person we encounter.

You could lose your health and ministry, have relationships broken and be overwhelmed and assaulted by spiritual attack, but if you truly know you are loved, and if you seek to be a lover, you will be successful in the sight of God.

I enjoy being successful in other realms, but I absolutely know that if nothing else happens and if everything else falls apart, I am already successful. Nobody can steal this from me. Nobody. The devil can't. Enemies can't. Friends can't.

Maintaining Your Confession As a Lover

I SPEAK THIS confession to God when I face pain and pressure: "I am loved, and I love You; therefore, I am successful. I love You even when my love is only in seed form and is still immature. Even though my love is weak, the position of my soul is to be a lover."

One reason why God allows pressure is because it refocuses our souls on reality. The pain of pressure drives our souls into the secret place.

When circumstances are difficult, many individuals hold to their confession that the circumstances will improve in a certain way. But a higher confession is this: I am loved, and I am a lover; therefore, I am successful. Pain will drive you to the only place of comfort—to that confession—the confession that delivers our hearts from despair.

When the pressure comes into my life, I hide in that secret place—in that posture of refocusing my soul. There I find the Spirit of Life, and I am quickened inside. It is like a muscle that is worked over and over. My heart keeps enlarging in the absolute truth that I am loved, I am a lover and therefore, I am successful.

No one can keep you from succeeding—no angry, jealous Saul—no hostile Philistine—no power of Satan. No one can keep me from being successful in the absolute definition that God gives of success.

Because the Son of God, the eternal heavenly Bridegroom, has chosen us as the delight of His heart, it is inconceivable that we would ever be insignificant. He has chosen us to rule and reign in that vast, eternal, expanding empire that is called the kingdom of God. We are what His heart pulsates for. We are what He longs for. We are what He waits for as His inheritance.

Knowing this, it is inconceivable that we would languish in the despair of insignificance. If only we could see who we are because of Him!

We can confidently say, "I may never have a big ministry, I may never have a big business and I may never be well recognized in the arenas of man, but I will never be insignificant. I am the one He loves. I am the one He died for. I am the one He longs for. I am the one He waits for."

Therefore, I can never be insignificant again—and neither can you!

I will seek the one I love.

—Song of Solomon 3:2

2

THE
BRIDEGROOM GOD

M Y FATHER WAS a professional boxer for eighteen years. As
an amateur boxer, he went to the Olympics and
became a world champion. I grew up in the gym around
cigar smoke, sweaty lockers, cheap bets and bloody fighters.
Later, my dad became entangled in the violent, criminal
underworld that surrounds the sport of boxing.

Dad trained me to box at the age of ten, and I loved leaving
the hot gym and going along with him to the neighborhood
bars where we were surrounded by street toughs and gang-
sters. You can imagine my initial dismay when God called me,
according to the Song of Solomon 8:6, to proclaim the message of Jesus as the heavenly Bridegroom and the passion of
the bride to the body of Christ.

It happened in July of 1998 as I was in my office praying.
This was one of the most defining experiences that I have
ever had in over twenty-five years with the Lord. At this
point, I knew little about the Song of Solomon, but during

this particular time of prayer and private devotion, I happened to be reading Song of Solomon 8:6–7. As I read the passage, the Spirit of God moved upon me, wooing me to God's love in a very unusual way. Deeply stirred, I began to weep, asking God to impart deep love for Jesus into my heart. The Spirit of the Lord rested on me in quiet power as I knelt in prayer. I have never experienced anything like this since that day.

I began to sense an intimacy with God that I had never before known. As the power of this experience intensified, I picked up the phone and asked the receptionist not to allow any calls to come to me. I didn't realize it at the time, but I was receiving my primary ministry commissioning as I gently wept, saying over and over, "Jesus, seal my heart; put Your own supernatural love in my heart. Put your fiery love in me."

Suddenly, I was startled as my phone rang. In a flash I went from being immersed in the Spirit of God to being upset. I took the call because it was from a good friend of mine. He began by informing me that he had a dream about me in which he heard the thunderous, audible voice of the Lord speaking the words of Song of Solomon 8:6–7. The Lord told him to call me and to give me a specific message.

First, he said that God told him that the Holy Spirit would emphasize the Song of Solomon, releasing its truth throughout the entire church and even to the entire earth in the coming generation. Second, he told me that the message of the Song of Solomon would become the focus of my life and ministry for the rest of my life. This was my ministry focus to call people back to the first commandment. Jesus said that the first and great commandment was that we should "love the LORD your God with all your heart, with all your soul, and with all your mind" (Matt. 22:37).

This initial experience left me stunned. Time went by quickly, and I thought, "Wow! What is this?" I have to confess that my first emotional reaction was one of dismay. The Song of Solomon seemed to me to be about roses and beauty and fragrance and flowers. I thought to myself, *This is horrible!* It was a love song, and I was actually a little bit discouraged about being called to proclaim this message for the rest of my life.

I even prayed, "Lord, I'm a boxer's son. I'm a tough guy's son! And now I'm called to be a bride of Christ guy?"

I was increasingly disturbed by the implications of this call as I pondered on it during the following days.

The Bride of
Christ Transcends Gender

AT THE TIME I didn't understand the significance of this message and ministry focus. I asked the Lord to give me a different type of ministry focus. I wanted a message that was more masculine. I suggested to God something deep and powerful like the Book of Romans, the Book of Revelation or the life of David. I wanted God to give me something that was manly! I figured that it would be better for God to give the Song of Solomon to a woman's ministry.

But in time, God changed my mind about this. I have learned that being the bride of Christ transcends gender. Indeed, men are the bride of Christ just as women are the sons of God. The bride describes a position of privilege and of nearness to the heart of God. It is an invitation to experience deep intimacy with God. Many men of God in the Bible walked in this exalted privilege of intimacy with God.

THE BRIDAL REVELATION

KING DAVID IS just one example of a man who was impacted by a life of deep intimacy with God. This is the essence of the bridal revelation that is developed theologically in the New Testament. In the Old Testament, King David was the ultimate worshiping warrior. I like to say that he was the king with a bride's heart. In other words, David was the picture of the lovesick worshiper in the Old Testament. John the Baptist, on the other hand, was the lovesick worshiper in the New Testament who actually saw the Bridegroom Himself.

However, the one who had the greatest revelation of the Bridegroom and the bride was the apostle John. At one point, this thunderous man wanted to call down fire from heaven on cities where people did not attend his meetings. John seemed to me on occasion to be out of control in the natural. Consider John's life. He rebuked people who cast out demons because they were not in his group. He asked Jesus to let him sit at His right hand forever. Imagine, he wanted to be the main guy over everyone forever at the right hand of Jesus in eternity. At times, this apostle rebuked people, but he was also the man who put his head on the Lord's breast.

The Lord Jesus entrusted the revelation of the bride to the apostle John, even beyond what He had revealed to John the Baptist. The apostle John, John the Baptist and David were all great men of God who were very much in touch with their own masculinity.

Many men think that understanding the bride of Christ undermines their masculinity, but just the opposite is true. In fact, the revelation of the bride will establish it. To be a man who lays His head on the Lord's breast and receives His embrace will set your heart ablaze.

A GOD WHO ENJOYS YOU

MOST OF US can believe that when we get to heaven that God will enjoy us there. Others picture a God who will enjoy them after they've experienced a significant spiritual transformation. But I have something stunning, radical and necessary to tell you: God enjoys you even now in your weakness. Whether you're up in victory or down in defeat—He still enjoys you, because His enjoyment of you is not based on your achievements but rather upon His own heart and your sincere response to Him. Whether you are struggling with difficulties or riding high, you are enjoyed by God Almighty.

As a matter of fact, feeling enjoyed by God on a regular basis will directly result in greater spiritual growth and maturity. This is not something for you to strive to achieve, but it is an awesome key that can unlock an amazing source of power in your life.

God also enjoys us in our weakness. I used to think that God could only enjoy me if I achieved a certain level of spiritual discipline and if I matured as a sincere believer. I now know this is not the case. Knowing that God enjoys me in my weakness actually leads to my spiritual maturity.

Some years ago the Lord showed me something profound that radically changed my life. The Lord showed me that because of the love in His own heart combined with the work of the cross, Jesus enjoyed me in my weakness. Really knowing this will cause us to mature—not the other way around.

My understanding of this continues to increase, particularly since God called me to the radiant and empowering message contained in the Song of Solomon. In fact, I believe God will revive the importance of this book across the earth, and as He does, it will change our understanding of God. I do not know of any book that changes our paradigm of God, line upon line, like the Song of Solomon.

The Song of Solomon can be understood in two main ways. First, it is a song that extols the beauty of natural, married love. Second, it is a spiritual love song about the glorious relationship of Christ and the church. According to this allegorical interpretation, King Solomon represents Christ the King, and the Shulamite is the bride of Christ. Understanding both the natural and allegorical interpretations is vital for Christians today.

We should approach this book as instruction for natural marriage on earth as well as gaining insight into our spiritual marriage as the bride of Christ. Both lead us to understand God's heart in a greater way.

GOD IS NOT A STRICT COACH

MANY BELIEVERS HAVE a very different view of God than the one described in this book of the Bible. If you press the average believer, he will say, "I know that God has total authority, and I know He means well, but I do not know how He feels. He seems a little distant in His emotions." God is often viewed as a strict coach who is trying to discipline us by calling us to hard things and by letting difficult things happen to us. We acknowledge that it is for our good; however, to view God as a coach is not an accurate understanding of His personality.

Others view Him as an exacting judge, always trying to catch us in our sin and never getting emotional until we fail—and then He gets angry.

Many of us look at God as a type of army sergeant who will sacrifice us for the sake of the cause. They see Him saying, "Oh well, it's OK if I lose a few along the way, so long as the cause goes forward." We think He calls us to be disciples just so His cause will be promoted, never realizing that His heart burns with desire for us. We also believe that He gets angry when we blow it. Beloved, this distortion is very different from the God of the Bible.

The Book of Psalms is closely related to Song of Solomon in how it carefully reveals the emotional makeup of the Godhead. Discovering God's heart is both fascinating and absolutely exhilarating!

SPIRITUAL PLEASURE GIVES US POWER OVER SIN

FOLLOWING MY PERSONAL sense of commissioning to proclaim the beauty of God from the Song of Solomon, I began my personal journey into the Song of Solomon. What happened in me and in my ministry occurred over the next several years. However, initially it took me completely by surprise. When I opened my Bible earlier that day to Song of Solomon 8:6-7, little did I realize that I would receive a phone call that very day that would change my life dramatically.

In this passage, Jesus is speaking. He invites the bride to set Him as a seal upon her heart and a seal upon her arm. This passage of Scripture says:

> Set me as a seal upon your heart,
> As a seal upon your arm;
> For love is as strong as death,
> Jealousy as cruel as the grave;
> Its flames are flames of fire,
> A most vehement flame.
> Many waters cannot quench love,
> Nor can the floods drown it.
> If a man would give for love
> All the wealth of his house,
> It would be utterly despised.

33

This passage reveals that God will impart His own love and jealousy within us that is as strong as death, and nothing can escape its grasp if we yield our hearts to it. Essentially, the Lord is saying that He has a love for us that burns like fire, despite our sin and brokenness. When we are yielded to the love of God, in time no sin or weakness can escape its grasp in the same way as nothing can escape the grasp of death in the natural realm.

It does not matter how much our hearts have been bitter or angry. It does not matter to what degree that we have sinned. The Lord can chase down such things. In the same way that death conquers everything in the natural, God's love conquers our hearts and overcomes sin that lives in our hearts. If we yield to His love, He can chase down the areas of our hearts that seem so prone to stray.

Toward the end of verse 6, the Lord begins to describe love's fire. It's with His fire of love that the Lord seals our hearts unto His own. These flames are like the flames of God—which function as a fiery seal. The seal with which God seals us unto Himself is not a wax seal like the seal that King Solomon used in his court to secure a royal document. Our hearts are the Lord's royal document, and He seals them with His own burning love.

It takes God to love God. We love Him with the supernatural power of His own imparted love. God will reveal His love and impart it to us, and we will become fiery lovers with His love. For God burns with desire for the human heart—He is the ultimate lover. He is not passive. That same burning desire is imparted to us and seals our hearts with fire. The icy waters of sin, bondage and persecution cannot extinguish this supernatural fire of God's love when we yield to its all-consuming power.

The Power to Love Is Its Own Reward

If a man would give for love all the wealth of his house,
it would be utterly despised.

—Song of Solomon 8:7

Picture a young couple with five million dollars in the bank who own a five-million-dollar house. One day this couple learns that their five-year-old daughter has a terminal illness. The doctor informs them that it will cost everything they have to successfully treat their child—their entire bank account, their home, their stocks—everything. So they liquidate their home and belongings and use all ten million dollars, and their daughter is saved. One day they meet someone who says, "That was incredible what you did for your daughter."

With a gentle rebuke the parents reply, "No, what we did for our daughter was nothing, because we did it for love." The same principle applies to this scripture. If a man has given up everything he has accumulated, he will despise the notion that it was somehow a noble act. He acted because he was totally preoccupied with the love of another. Next to such love, money has no value. He might answer such a question as follows: "I consider what I gave up to be worthless compared to the love I have for my daughter."

The apostle Paul said that he considered his sacrifice for Christ as rubbish compared to the excellency of experiencing the beauty of Jesus. (See Philippians 3:8.) The people said to him, "Paul, you had such a brilliant career." To Paul it meant nothing when weighed against what the Savior gave for Him. The uncreated God became human because He burned with a desire for us. He crowns us with His eternal glory. So what if Paul gave up a would-be-famous career? True love despises the recognition for sacrifices made for love.

Why? Because it was the sacrifice of love. The reward of a true lover is the power to love. At this point of love, no self-recognition is sought or wanted.

In essence, the parents in our illustration were saying, "We love our daughter, and that is all that matters; the house and money mean nothing." In the same manner, when men and women are so preoccupied with the love and beauty of Jesus, the power to respond in wholehearted love toward God is the only reward they want. Martyrs will gladly give their lives and see their act of supreme devotion as God's gift of grace to them, which enables them to operate in supernatural love under pressure. The power to love is our great reward.

ROMANCED WARRIORS ARE
PROTECTED AND EMPOWERED

WHEN GOD CALLED me to begin seeing myself through the revelation of the bride of Christ, I protested. How could the son of a tough boxer focus on proclaiming to the body of Christ about being a bride? Confused, I said, "Lord, that does not make sense!"

Now I understand that I will never enter into a more radical posture as a warrior than as a bridal warrior, a romanced warrior against the kingdom of darkness. In this posture we will be secure, and our heart will be protected. We will have power to sustain us in the battle. Other warriors will burn out, they'll get injured and the passion in their hearts will be lost.

It is so easy to get your heart wounded in the heat of battle. But romanced warriors' hearts are more protected and empowered because they carry their primary reward (which is the power to be exhilarated in love and fascinated with beauty) within their hearts. Though they may even die as martyrs, their hearts die aflame with the passion of Christ's love. I believe that the End-Time church is going to be a romanced warrior, a bridal warrior. Jesus' bride has on army boots, and she is a bride whose heart is protected by enjoying love. Today's John the Baptists, King Davids and Sons of Thunder need to get into the bridal revelation.

Although my first response to my call to the Song of Solomon was one of dismay, I soon realized the power of this experience with the Lord. That's when I told the Lord, "Let's do it!"

I will admit that it took me a while to resolve my questions about this. But it did not take me long to decide that I'd best not wrestle with God, since I knew that He would win anyway. Having lost every wrestling match I ever had with God, after a few weeks I said, "OK."

So I went and bought books on the Song of Solomon. I started reading them, and honestly, I found some of them uninteresting and confusing. It took diligence and faith. There are really only about fifteen different symbols in the Song of Solomon, and once you learn them they work. It is not really that difficult, but with no knowledge of the symbols, at first it seemed nearly impossible. I now own about 150 commentaries on the Song of Solomon. I have a goal to get every commentary in English on this that I can get my hands on.

I began to pray and fast, asking the Lord to unlock this book of the Bible. Soon, my study of the Song of Solomon began to delight my heart more and more. And now, twelve years later, I feel that I have only begun to study this powerful book. Some have dedicated fifty years to studying this one book of the Bible. I have taught the Song of Solomon year after year in our full-time Bible school in Kansas City. Today, it is truly an unspeakable delight to me. My delight is not just in preaching it, but little by little my heart is becoming unlocked as I prepare, study and meditate on these passages of Scripture. I believe that the Song of Solomon is essential to the forerunner ministry, to the romanced warrior whose heart is protected by experiencing Jesus' love and beauty.

Many dimensions of His beauty and our beauty are linked to the revelation of this book, the paradigm of a God who is an affectionate Bridegroom overcome with desires. I will briefly cover three points of this enormous weight of revelation contained within the pages of this powerful book of the Bible.

JESUS THE BRIDEGROOM DESIRES US

WHEN I CONSIDER God the Bridegroom, I first think about His desire for us. Oh, to be exhilarated with God's love! Nothing is more invigorating than the revelation of the God filled with pleasure, the God who has intense desire for human beings and the God who woos us through spiritual pleasures. There are many implications to this new paradigm of God the Son as a Bridegroom God in His humanity.

The revelation of the Bridegroom was preached by the apostle Paul. He said:

> For I am jealous for you with godly jealousy. *For I have betrothed you to one husband,* that I may present you as a chaste virgin to Christ.
> —2 CORINTHIANS 11:2, EMPHASIS ADDED

Paul saw his ministry as betrothing unbelievers through conversion to a Bridegroom God and presenting them as a pure bride. In this ministry identity, namely as friends of the

38

Bridegroom, we operate very differently than those without this revelation. Friends of the Bridegroom are fearless because we are connected to something far bigger than ourselves. We get our identity through the power of relationship with God Himself.

A Bridegroom God is a God who has indescribable desire and delight in human beings. He is a God in whom we feel liked, enjoyed, wanted, pursued and delighted. Something resonates in us when we feel the burning desire of God's heart.

Both the Father and the Bridegroom desire us. The Holy Spirit, on the other hand, mediates this revelation and imparts love to our hearts so that we might respond wholeheartedly to the Father as children and to the Son of God as a bride.

Whether our hearts are focused on the Father God or the Bridegroom God, we experience burning desire. Something profound happens in us when even in our weakness and brokenness we feel wanted, longed for and rejoiced in. Our response is to abandon our hearts to God. When we see Him as our Bridegroom, our need to feel enjoyed by God is met. Our lives and personalities are completely changed by the realization that God not only likes us and enjoys us in heaven, but He actually enjoys us and takes pleasure in us while we are here on the earth.

RUN TO HIM

THERE IS NO greater declaration of unrelenting desire, love and passion than a Bridegroom God who took upon Himself the form of a man because He wanted a marriage partner forever. In doing this, He glorifies the Father. When I think of my Bridegroom God, my heart says, "Stunning desire!" He is a God who desires me beyond anything I imagine. I will run to

Him instead of from Him the moment I understand that.

When you have the revelation of the Bridegroom God, you do not retreat from Him when you consider your sinful flesh. Instead, you run to Him. You run to Him because you know the type of God He is. Of course, we must have a sincere and willing spirit. Here, I am referring to genuine believers who are struggling in their sin, but their hearts cry out to be different. Their heart's cry is, "I want to be Yours—yet, I discover my weakness so often."

THE BEAUTY REALM

BEAUTY IS THE second word I think of when referring to the Bridegroom. The beauty realm of God is opened to us by the Spirit of God. This will happen in an unprecedented way in the generation in which the Lord returns. We will be stunned and fascinated by the unveiling of a beautiful God.

He imparts the very beauty He possesses. He imparts it through redemption. Without understanding the paradigm of a Bridegroom God, we cannot fully understand the revelation of His beauty. He intends to show us this fullness in this age in which we live. The revelation of the Bridegroom God is essential to fulfill the purposes of God during this last age.

The Bridegroom God is such a vast subject. My life is an eager treasure hunt into this dimension of God's heart. I have followed hard after this revelation for the last twelve years, and I cannot wait for God to unfold more of the beauty realm to me over the next twelve years. The closer I get to it, the happier I become in holiness. Oh, to be fascinated with His beauty!

HIS PLANS FOR US

THE THIRD CONCEPT I think of when I consider the Bridegroom

God is His plans for us. God has called you and me to share some of the glorious inheritance that He receives from His Father. He has called us into a place of intimacy and power that actually is far beyond the angels. He plans for redeemed people to enter into a realm with the Godhead that is far beyond any other created thing.

I love being human, and I love being alive! I can't wait to get to heaven. There could not possibly be a greater deception than the lie that says this life is not worth living. Life is absolutely wonderful. Just think of it! There is a Bridegroom God who has plans to share intimacy and power with us. He is a Bridegroom God who is ravished over His new bride—us.

Revelation 3:21 is a powerful statement from the very lips of Jesus describing what we will inherit. Here the Lord tells how He desires for us to sit on His throne with Him.

> To him who overcomes I will grant to sit with Me on My
> throne, as I also overcame and sat down with My Father
> on His throne.

Beloved, you have married into indescribable wealth and power and into the aristocracy of the eternal city. One day soon you will instantly be in the midst of it in full power.

Giving our hearts to Him as voluntary lovers is the only purpose God has for us. Therefore, that should be the summation and summary of all that we are and all that we do. When we receive our crown on the last day, we will then say, "We have loved You because we so enjoyed loving You. We were not forced to love You. This is how we long to live. We did not serve out of some sort of mandatory decree of obedience. We are voluntary lovers of God. We want to be lovers because of the beauty of God."

41

To be wholehearted lovers of God is the focus of the fore-runner ministry, a call that is very dear to my heart. (See Matthew 22:37.) Forerunners are those who experience intimacy with a heavenly Bridegroom God who calls His people to abandonment and to the romance of the gospel.

Developing our relationship with the Bridegroom God is the best way we will know the fullness of His plan for us. Being a voluntary lover of the Bridegroom God, coming into greater revelation of what that means will radically change our priorities and every aspect of our lives. Our destiny as His bride is set before us even now.

"And it shall be, in that day,"
Says the LORD,
"That you will call Me 'My Husband,'
And no longer call Me 'My Master.'"

—Hosea 2:16

3

RESTORING THE
FIRST COMMANDMENT

A S A TEENAGER, I always enjoyed watching my brother Pat. As an excellent athlete, he grew up succeeding.

But about twenty-seven years ago, in the middle of an intense football game, the unthinkable happened. The loud speaker called out my brother's number above the confusion of screaming fans and the scramble of coaches, players and friends. Pat had been severely injured. Since that awful moment he has spent the last twenty-seven years of his life lying on his back, completely paralyzed from the injuries of that game.

Because my brother is totally paralyzed, I have spent a lot of time hanging around hospitals—especially in the early years. Every now and then I have watched as something very interesting happens. I have noticed that when a nurse falls in love with her patient, suddenly, the nurse becomes the lover. No longer is she just a worker, for a powerful transformation has taken place. She no longer watches the clock. She cares little about her salary. She no longer goes down a checklist of duties to perform. Now that she has become a lover the checklist is stamped in her heart. It's truly fascinating to watch what happens when the nurse becomes a bride. Indeed, when the worker becomes a lover, the dynamic between the two individuals completely changes.

Lovers will always serve more willingly and easily than workers ever will. We can see this concept in Hosea 2:16.

> "And it shall be in that day,"
> Says the LORD,
> "That you will call Me 'My Husband,'
> And no longer call Me 'My Master.'"

This verse speaks of a time at the end of the age when the spirit of revival will cover God's people, and they will speak of their relationship with the Lord in an entirely different way. They will call Him their Husband rather than their Master. As servants, they will still obey Him, but the servitude of workers will be replaced with the joy and energy of lovers whose passion and joy are to please the One who is the object of their love.

This scripture says "in that day," referring to the end of this age when the spirit of revival will be poured upon both the nation of Israel and the body of Christ worldwide. We will not be preoccupied by duty. We will experience more than a servant/Master relationship; we will work and serve more diligently. We will actually obey God in a more intense way. We will call Him our Husband because we will see ourselves as His bride.

Working Lovers, Not Loving Workers

GOD WANTS YOU to be a lover. And He wants you to be a working lover. Who you are is the lover, and what you do is the work. You are not to be only a worker who struggles to love God. Instead, you are a lover of God.

Being lovers is our very identity. It's who we are. We are lovers of God who happen to work, not the other way around. God wants us to be something *before* He wants us to do something. In a fallen world, we want to do something in order to be someone. With God, exactly the opposite is true. God wants us to be lovers so that we do work.

It is extremely important that what we do flows out of who we are. It is also important that we do not live from the self-centered motivation of trying to be something and seeking to achieve more. With minds that are not renewed, we work to feel important and to appear significant in the eyes of others. God expects just the opposite of that. We are not first warriors; we are first a bride. We are first lovers, and then we do the acts of war.

God wants us to be relationally oriented first and achievement oriented second. Yes, we are to do the Great Commission, but who we are in Him is far more important than what we do for Him. In fact, who we are will dramatically impact what we do. Christ's kingdom is established in this way. He does indeed want us to sow spiritual seed and cultivate a spiritual garden. To know we are loved, to actually feel God's affection, is more vital to our growth to be a wholehearted lover of God. This is our life source. This is the essence of true success. Once we are successful in this spiritual sense, then we can serve Him in ministry with deeper obedience and perseverance. He cares a great deal about productivity, but He cares about it second. Too many of us put it first. He wants us to be loved and a lover first, and then He wants us to disciple the nations, starting with our families and with our neighbors.

When we are relationally oriented first, we do not work in ministry because of a need to feel successful. We already feel successful because of our relationship with Jesus. We launch out and do the work of the Great Commission from a foundation of success. This sense of success equips us to continue working even when we face adversity. But if we work because we are trying to achieve success, we will burn out quickly through added temptation and strife.

THOU SHALT LOVE THE LORD

> Jesus said unto him, Thou shalt love the Lord thy God with all thy heart, and with all thy soul, and with all thy mind. This is the first and great commandment. And the second is like unto it, Thou shalt love thy neighbour as thyself. On these two commandments hang all the law and the prophets.
>
> —MATTHEW 22:37–40, KJV

Of course, it's absolutely essential for us to embrace Christ's mandate to reach out to people and to touch the nations. But this heart of service must be secondary, not primary. The reversal of these priorities was Martha's problem. Let's look:

> Now it happened as they went that He entered a certain village; and a certain woman named Martha welcomed Him into her house. And she had a sister called Mary, who also sat at Jesus' feet and heard His word. But Martha was distracted with much serving, and she approached Him and said, "Lord, do You not care that my sister has

left me to serve alone? Therefore tell her to help me."

And Jesus answered and said to her, "Martha, Martha, you are worried and troubled about many things. But one thing is needed, and Mary has chosen that good part, which will not be taken away from her."

—LUKE 10:38-42

When Mary and Martha were in their little conflict, Martha was not wrong because she wanted to be a servant. However, her priorities were upside down because her natural self, her natural abilities and interests compelled her to be a worker before she was a lover. In fact, her work distracted her from being a lover (v. 40).

Martha was doing much more that was right than wrong. Unlike Martha, many people are neither lovers nor servers of God. Rather than having either of these two commandments as the focus of their hearts, many Christians are consumed with self.

When I encounter somebody whose focus is based on reaching out to others, I applaud the grace of God in that individual because at least he or she has moved out of being self-absorbed and now cares enough to be a worker. It's good to be a worker. I am a worker in God's kingdom. However, I am neither primarily nor only a worker for God. I praise God for hard-working brothers and sisters because so many believers are only focused on receiving personal blessings. In fact, many individuals are so focused on enriching their earthly circumstances and pursuing personal comforts that they never get serious about becoming a worker, let alone a lover. When I see a worker I say to myself, "Well, he's halfway there." But I also understand that such an individual will be a much more effective worker if he or she first becomes a lover.

Are you a student of the Bible? It is important for us to remember that although it is good to study the Word of God, we are not called to be students first. I love to study the Scriptures, but I am not first called to be a student. I am first called to be a lover. Oh, the glory of being a lover of God! I love to love Him! Therefore, I study in a way that produces love in my heart and produces love in the hearts of the people I impact. Depending on an individual's heart, being a student can either help or hinder a person to fulfill this first priority.

On this same note, we are not called primarily to be debaters or fighters for truth. Some people think that their mandate in life is to preserve the truth. They do not realize that we are first called to be lovers. Yes, God wants us to fight for truth, but never before we wrestle with the idea of being lovers of God.

We are also not called to be religious. We are not called primarily to jump through the hoops of our religious systems and political structures, or to dot the *i* and to cross the *t* according to a particular doctrine or policy. He has called us first to be lovers.

The Great Commission was spoken from the heart of our Father God to a bride who is ordained to partner with the Son of God. It was spoken to the church to be a lover partner, whose work would flow out of the energy of divine romance through hearts energized with love. The Great Commission is often seen through the paradigm of a worker. It is seen as a mandate of great sacrifice. But by the end of the age, evangelism will be accomplished as the overflow of a lover in partnership with her Bridegroom God. We won't consider it sacrifice, but a privilege. We will work in the fields of harvest with hearts that are absolutely lovesick with desire for the Lord of the Harvest.

Currently, we view evangelism through the grid of missionary sacrifice: We surrender our lives as the cost of service. This understanding is certainly legitimate, but it's just not the highest paradigm of the Great Commission. Jesus talked about counting the cost. But don't forget that Jesus only asked new believers to do this. He invited those who were uninstructed in the grace of God, whose minds were not yet renewed.

Sacrifice is not the primary consideration for those who have been touched by the romance of the gospel, whose hearts are stirred by the beauty of God and who have a deep reality of love for God. Instead, such believers are caught up in the privilege of abandonment. Their primary reward is the power to love. Their reward is to feel and receive love, and then to reciprocate it by the power of God. They carry this reward within their hearts.

Therefore, the Great Commission will move from a work paradigm of sacrificial labor to a love paradigm, an act of devotion of a lovesick bride. In this new paradigm, we carry our reward in our hearts because the first commandment is first.

BEING A LOVER STARTS RIGHT AWAY

WE CAN HAVE a lover's heart before we have ever mastered any of the disciplines. Having a heart to be a lover is initiated by the Spirit of God at the new birth in Christ. It is the seed of a lover in us that cries, "Abba, Father." It is a gift of God given to us on the day of our new birth in Christ. Before we change one single habit of our lives, a lover's cry is there within us.

> And because you are sons, God has sent forth the Spirit
> of His Son into your hearts, crying out, "Abba, Father!"
> —GALATIANS 4:6

It's important for us to realize how easily distracted we can become. In fact, even before we begin to work on the disciplines of the Christian life, that cry of a lover is easily quenched. But if we just get quiet, we will feel the rumblings of the lover's cry deep in our spirits—"Abba, Father. Abba, Father."

AVOIDING BURNOUT

MANY CHRISTIANS WHO reach out to others burn out quickly because they launch out into ministry before they establish in themselves the foundations of being lovers of God. Discouragement, despair, boredom and frustration will inevitably occur if we do not recognize that we are first called to be lovers. Yes, God has called us to be workers. Yes, we are called to be servants. Yes, we are called to bear the inconveniences of being caregivers to other people. But we must remember that such works of service are a part of the second commandment; they are an overflow of the first commandment.

What happens when we want to first be workers or fighters for the truths of our particular religious system? What happens if we first want to be students or to disciple others? What happens when our first priority is to fulfill the Great Commission to go into all the world and preach the gospel to every creature? (See Mark 16:15.)

Devastating things can happen when we place ministry to others and the Great Commission as first in our lives.

The first thing to go wrong is burnout. When we are lovers first, when the first commandment is first, our sacrifice and labor are rewarded. This reward is twofold:

• The Holy Spirit communicates to us that God loves us.

- We become a vessel through which the Father's love for Jesus flows through us back to Him.

This twofold reward keeps us invigorated, and therefore, we avoid much of the burnout so common today.

God fashioned us to receive love and to be vessels through which His affection flows back to Him. Therefore, it just feels right when we experience His love in our moments of weakness and distress. At such times we can have the Father's affection and enjoyment for Jesus pulsating through our hearts back to God.

The reward of our labor is that we get to enjoy being a lover as the primary preoccupation of our lives. It's a pleasure beyond compare. But we suffer greatly when we are workers first. When workers are mistreated, when the anointing of God does not show up as we want or when circumstances disappoint us, we have nothing to fall back on—except waiting for heaven. The result of such pressure is usually burnout.

But the outcome is far different for lovers. As a lover first, now when I experience attacks from other people, when I am undermined, when things don't work out, when disappointment comes while I am laboring for the gospel, I can always run back to the secret place. I still have a secret place of pleasure where I am immersed in the knowledge that God loves me. This is where God imparts back to me a little bit of the Father's love for His Son. This is true spiritual pleasure!

PLEASURES IN GOD REDUCE BURNOUT

GOD HAS ORDAINED many pleasures for believers. There are physical, emotional and intellectual pleasures, all of which are ordained by God. But no pleasure is more intense than the pleasure that comes when God communicates Himself to the human spirit. In the little moments when God communicates His passion for me, I experience what life is all about. It is life at its very best.

Such tender moments with God cause life and spiritual vitality to resonate deep within. Of course, we do not experience an unbroken sense of God's love in this life. Such dramatic touches of God's presence tend to wane. Only in heaven will we enjoy the continual ecstasy of His presence. But during my tender moments with God in this life, I say to myself and to God, "Oh, yes, I like life. Life is good!"

As God pours His love into me, that same love flows through me back to Him. As I am loving Him back, greater revelation of His affection and beauty comes to me, and the cycle just gets richer and richer. Just like anyone else, I am a regular person, saved and kept by grace. I experience seasons of spiritual pleasure, and then I go through times of dryness and dullness wherein I get mad, glad, sad and feel all of the other human emotions.

But burnout occurs when we do not experience the pleasure of the Christian life found in a love relationship with God. I try to be careful not to exaggerate the intensity of such encounters with the Holy Spirit, for I don't want to encourage you to reach for a particular experience instead of seeking after God Himself and letting Him reveal Himself to you as an individual. This is important because getting focused on unrealistic spiritual expectations can actually lead to feeling condemned and discouraged, and leave you doubting whether God loves you or not.

However, feeling loved—a little bit—and feeling love for God—a little bit—has a powerfully dynamic impact upon the human spirit. I don't cry out this message because I want to be a noble soldier for God. I'm committed to sharing this message, to crying out the necessity of putting the first commandment first because I've experienced a reality that the body of Christ has within its reach. But we must refocus our souls; we must put first things first to realize the awesome spiritual pleasures of walking in a love relationship with Christ.

LIVING BY LOVE

HIS EMBRACES HAVE staying power in our lives. Even the remembrance of His past embraces holds me steady when I go for weeks or months at a time without a fresh encounter of His love. In dry times, when the heavens feel like brass, I remember the seasons when I have felt His embrace. The memory of the splendor and pleasure of past intimacy with Jesus keeps me going. Admittedly I do not like dry seasons, and I resist them. But after awhile I realize that my dry seasons can help me to grow. I recognize that dryness is used by God to strengthen me for the future. In His love and tender mercy, God has shown me that along with needing His embrace, I also need times of dryness. I need both of these to mature properly.

Living by love and finding strength in God's embrace will revolutionize your Christian life. For people who are in love quit a lot less than people who are not in love. When a person is in love, he simply does not give up nearly as easily. Being in love will prop us up and strengthen us when we're tempted to let go.

BEING A LOVER REDUCES TEMPTATION

BEING A LOVER of God not only reduces burnout, but it also reduces temptation. This is because satisfied people sin less. Much of the sin in the body of Christ is a wrong response to pain, fear and the need for comfort. Sin is a false comfort that people use as a prop to get them through seasons of pain. Many people get into sin because they feel beaten up and abandoned by God and men. Even though they are not truly abandoned, they feel that way. So they reach out for immediate comfort in status, financial gain or wrong expressions of sexuality. Although they are not sinless, spiritually satisfied people do sin less.

BEING A LOVER REDUCES STRIFE

HAPPY PEOPLE ALSO fight less. I get beat up by rejection and criticism just as everybody else does. I even get beat up by believers who say false and evil things about me. These attacks come from people close to me and also from people whom I have never even met.

I do not always respond positively to such attacks, even when I am in a season in which I am sensing the communion of the Holy Spirit. But when I have that little bit of happiness that comes from feeling the embrace of God, I fight people a whole lot less.

It reminds me of how I felt when I first met my wife. I was so lovesick with infatuation that if some guy had stolen my car, I would have said, "You can have my car. And here, do you want my wallet, too?" Satisfied people just fight less.

The body of Christ simply will not function properly until the first commandment is where it is supposed to be, in first place. This is absolutely imperative to the health of the body of Christ. I appreciate people whose number one drive is the Great Commission and relationships. But I also know that until being a lover of God becomes their first priority, they will burn out, be tempted and become entangled in strife.

DRIVEN BY LOVE

THE APOSTLE PAUL said, "The love of Christ constraineth us" (2 Cor. 5:14, KJV). The word *constrain* means "to grip tightly." Paul was motivated by Christ's love working in him and through him. God's love became a driving force in all he did. It is the very power of living in godliness. I encourage people to focus on enjoying God more, not trying harder to overcome sin.

Many people are driven by fear instead of by affection for God. In fact, I often recognize fear in many of my friends. I even see it in my own heart at times. When fear comes, we must respond by throwing ourselves into the first commandment. I become far more stable on the second commandment and the Great Commission when the first commandment is first in my life. The wonder, freedom, power and pleasure of this is within the reach of every Christian, because it is the work of the Holy Spirit in the human spirit.

The Holy Spirit pours out God's very affection into the human heart regardless of our personality type or history of bondage, regardless of where we've been wounded or how we've been broken. It's a supernatural activity that transcends the human condition.

> Now hope does not disappoint, because the love of God
> has been poured out in our hearts by the Holy Spirit
> who was given to us.
>
> —ROMANS 5:5

As we position our souls to make the first commandment first, we will be lovers before we are workers. We will be worshipers before we are warriors. Through Christ's loving embrace, He will show us that we are to be a bride before we are an army.

57

THE CHERISHING MINISTRY OF CHRIST

NOT ONLY IS the first commandment most attacked by Satan, it is also most neglected by the body of Christ. Satan's attacks come in a strategic way. Immediately following the passage of Scripture in which Paul speaks of presenting the church as a chaste virgin to Christ, he speaks of his concern that the carnal Corinthian church might be deceived by Satan.

> But I am afraid, lest as the serpent deceived Eve by his craftiness, your minds should be led astray from the simplicity and purity of devotion to Christ.
> —2 CORINTHIANS 11:3, NAS

Paul was speaking to the Corinthians when he said that Jesus had betrothed them to one husband as a pure, chaste virgin. This had nothing to do with their ability or their performance. It was based completely on the fact that they were born again. By virtue of the new birth, they were presented to the Lord Jesus as a bride, as a pure virgin, to a Husband. Paul's words were spoken to the Corinthians, the most carnal church in the entire New Testament writings. What a distinction! Satan doesn't want you presented to Jesus as His bride. He'd love to undermine this process. His strategy is to sidetrack you and to divert you from the simplicity of undistracted love and devotion.

Satan attacks us by undermining our revelation of God. When we lose the revelation of Him as our Bridegroom, we forget His tenderness, His embrace and His kindness to us. Then when we do not feel cherished by Him in our weakness, we begin to be distracted from pure devotion.

Ephesians 5:27 says, "That He might present her to Himself a glorious church, not having spot or wrinkle or any such thing, but that she should be holy and without blemish." Jesus presents a church to Himself that is full of glory. One day the church will be presented to the Lord Jesus via His own work. He actually presents the church to Himself.

In other words, He does this by the work of His own death upon the cross. You may wonder how this happens. We can see how this takes place in Ephesians 5:29: "For no one ever hated his own flesh, but nourishes and cherishes it, just as the Lord does the church." Jesus "nourishes and cherishes" the church in the same way a man does his wife.

The power of having a nourished heart and the exhilaration of a cherished heart—this is the very wellspring of life!

I believe a time will come when the church is full of glory and an explosive release of the cherishing ministry of Christ Jesus will sweep over the people of God. Jesus has shown Himself to Paul the Apostle as the Husband who will cherish a weak, broken church. Indeed, Paul says Christ cherishes the church as a man living by the Spirit of God will cherish his wife. A man walking in the flesh does not love his wife in this way, but a spiritual man will cherish his wife as Jesus cherishes the church. Jesus does not just teach the church. He does not just comfort the church. He does not just guide the church. He actually embraces and cherishes her as a loving husband cherishes his wife.

I believe the Song of Solomon is an essential strategy of God for revealing the cherishing ministry of Jesus. The cherishing ministry is an outpouring of a divine Husband's love upon the church. As this powerful revelation is experienced by believers throughout the body of Christ, a divine passion will flow from the bride back to the Lord. This powerful outpouring will reach its height in the generation when the glorious church is presented. I believe it will come with the revelation of the Bridegroom.

Jesus is not just the Lord of the harvest, but He is also the Lord of the Sabbath. In other words, He is the Lord of sitting at the feet of Jesus as Mary did. He is also the Lord of intimate moments with God.

The true spiritual Sabbath rest is a time that is set aside to give our hearts to God. Mary of Bethany did this as she sat at the feet of Jesus. Giving our hearts to the Lord is the fulfillment of the Sabbath. The Sabbath is not taking time off of work to rest. Instead, the Sabbath rest is having our whole hearts immersed in God. Though it also serves the dual purpose of giving us physical rest, the highest purpose of the Sabbath is to engage our hearts in an undistracted way.

RESTORING THE FIRST
COMMANDMENT TO FIRST PLACE

THE BRIDEGROOM'S PASSION, His burning desire for human beings, the beauty He possesses that we hardly understand—a vast ocean of reality and revelation about the God-Man, Christ Jesus, exists that the Spirit of God will reveal at the end of the age. It will be the glory and the strength of the End-Time church. I believe the Holy Spirit's strategy in these hours is to raise up men and women to whom He will release a forerunner calling. The forerunner ministry is very significant for the end of the age. I will examine this ministry in future chapters.

The Holy Spirit will restore the first commandment to first place, because the first commandment is the great commandment. Right now, in my estimation, the first commandment is only ranked among the top ten in the church today. Christians think about it once in a while, sometimes they may refer to it, occasionally they may pray about it, here and there they may yield to it, but the first commandment is nowhere close to being the first priority in the body of Christ at large. I am not worried, however; it will be first before Jesus returns.

There are several levels of reward. In fact, secondary rewards on the earth are very important. They include an anointed ministry, a breakthrough of finances, a couple of good friends, health and strength. All of these are very important rewards, but they are secondary. I love the secondary rewards. We need them, and they are God's will.

When the first commandment is seen as a task of labor, as a sacrifice, the secondary rewards often become primary to us. In other words, our main concern becomes how much anointing is on our ministry, how much money we have, the condition of our health, the number of deep and loyal friendships we have. These secondary rewards become our primary focus when we see ourselves as making sacrifices for God. However, such rewards become secondary when Jesus is our magnificent obsession, because our highest level of purpose is fulfilled.

We become powerful and fearless in the grace of God when the primary purpose of love for which we were created begins to be fulfilled. This is the anointing of the first commandment. And we carry our love as our reward with us wherever we go, even during dry seasons.

IDENTIFIED AS A LOVER

WE ARE LOVED by Him, and therefore, we are lovers of Him. That is our primary identity. From this perspective, life looks totally different because no matter what happens, a song fills our hearts, our spirits are stirred and our inner man becomes tender toward God.

61

I have set out to do risky ministry endeavors that the Lord called me to and have unexpectedly hit many brick walls. I have also had my words fall to the ground as I was preaching when the heavens seemed like brass. I know what it's like to go into a prayer meeting a little bit happy and to leave depressed. I know about ministry endeavors in which I felt as if I had lost ground, even though I knew I was in the will of God.

During such times the Lord makes clear to me that He does not want ministry or financial success to be our primary reward. He wants His Son to be our magnificent obsession, not the fact that we might preach to a stadium of 100,000 people and lead ten thousand to the Lord. Sure, preaching to thousands and winning people to Christ is good, but even that has to be our secondary reward.

The great news is that when your primary reward is in place, you can be in prison and still be successful. You can have the disappointments of a lifetime in your ministry and have people in the local church misunderstand you and write you off, but you will still be successful in your heart if loving Him and being loved by Him is your primary reward.

JESUS PRAYS FOR THE FIRST COMMANDMENT TO BE FIRST

IN JOHN 17, Jesus prays the high priestly prayer that ends His ministry. Next, He goes to the Garden of Gethsemane and finally to the cross. The priestly prayer is the greatest intercessory prayer in the Word of God. It is one of the longest intercessory prayers recorded in the Bible. Every single phrase is filled with volumes of meaning. For the last time in the flesh, the Son of God is praying in the will of God while under the power of the Holy Spirit.

This prayer lives forever making a lasting intercessory cry for the church.

Everything that Jesus prayed for our future is a promise that cannot fail. He did not pray amiss; everything the Lord asked from the Father in this prayer will come to pass. I think it should be the prayer of prayers, the model prayer in our desire to grow in intercession. Ask the Spirit of God to reveal John 17 to you.

The way in which Jesus ends the prayer is amazingly profound. In John 17:26, He says:

> And I have declared to them Your name, and will declare
> it, that the love with which You loved Me may be in
> them, and I in them.

In this passage, the Lord Jesus offers a final cry as the earthly High Priest. Essentially, Jesus says to the Father, "You said there would be a people who would love Me as You love Me, Father." In essence, Jesus asks the Father to supernaturally impart the Father's love for the Son into us, therefore creating voluntary lovers who are so ravished with love that it can only be compared to the way the Father loves Christ.

Before the world has ended, the first commandment will dominate and prevail in the lives of God's people worldwide. The Father's holy zeal for His Son will fill the hearts of God's people.

This prayer of intercession was Jesus' gift to the church. Just try to imagine the effect of an affection for and a fascination with Jesus that is the overflow of the love that the Father has for His Son. That is what Jesus prayed for us to receive.

THE SPIRIT AND THE BRIDE

The Spirit and the bride say, "Come!"

—REVELATION 22:17

In this passage of Scripture the people of God see the Son of God, the Son of Man—fully God and fully man. They see Him in a way that they have never before understood Him. They see Him as a heavenly Bridegroom. And from the overflow of that revelation, they see themselves in an entirely new light as a cherished, lovesick bride. This new spiritual identity changes our emotional chemistry. It changes everything about us. When the Holy Spirit and the church are in unity in a bridal identity, together we will cry out, "Come!"

The Holy Spirit is at work today revealing the Bridegroom God to us. As the Holy Spirit reveals to God's people the attributes and character of the Bridegroom, lovers will rise up to wholehearted devotion. This revelation of the Bridegroom God will empower, sustain, shield and protect the Bride during the difficult times that lie ahead.

FOR THE LORD YOUR GOD IS A CONSUMING FIRE, A
JEALOUS GOD.

—DEUTERONOMY 4:24

4

THE FIRE OF GOD
IN HOLY ROMANCE

THERE IS NOTHING more compelling or attractive than desire that goes above and beyond. Hollywood has made billions of dollars from the craving of the human heart to experience deep, abiding love. The love stories through the ages are very similar. They are the stories of the man who sells all to win the love of his lady. People flock to the theater to see the same story line over and over. Why? Because something in us longs for love that knows no boundaries, love that knows no sacrifice in pursuit of the one it loves. Shakespeare's timeless classic *Romeo and Juliet* touches the deep chord within. It cries out that life itself is only worthwhile if the heart burns with love. There is no sacrifice too great when the heart is set on fire.

When you understand the revelation of the fire of God, experiencing His burning desire for His Son and for other human beings will radically change your life. I love how in Song of Solomon 7:10, the bride says, "His desire is toward me." What a statement! Out of a heart consumed with fiery love the bride proclaims, "I am my beloved's, and his desire is toward me."

As God opens the treasure chest contained in that scripture, we will see how the power of that revelation will be ours here on earth, not just in heaven. We can rest in the confession that His desire burns for us. The transcendent, uncreated God who stands outside of time is moved with desire and is planning glorious things for you and me.

The Bible says:

> But as it is written, Eye hath not seen, nor ear heard, nei-
> ther have entered into the heart of man, the things
> which God hath prepared for them that love him.
> —1 CORINTHIANS 2:9, KJV

FIERY, JEALOUS DESIRE

MANY PEOPLE THINK that a burning God is a God filled with wrath and anger, destroying everything in His path. However, God burns with a radiant heart of intense desire. Yes, this God of intense desire destroys everything that hinders love, but His fire is first about His pleasure and His holy romance with His people.

In Deuteronomy 4:24 it is evident that Moses understands the burning God here: "For the LORD your God is a consuming fire, a jealous God." God's fire of judgment is an overflow, a sub-department of His fire of burning desire for His people. It is a manifestation of passion that removes everything that hinders love. Does sin hinder love? God will judge it in fiery passion to free His bride. Do enemies assault the people of God? Judgment will come upon the devil and his forces as God is stirred with fiery passion to protect His beloved. God will judge His enemies because of fiery love. His heart will be increasingly stirred with fiery jealousy, and He will strike His enemies to protect and avenge His bride.

This might be difficult to comprehend at the present time, but one day some of us will come forth as trumpeters, or proclaimers, of the romance of the gospel in a way that we do not expect. Over time the seeds of desire planted deep in our spirit-man will grow. They have certainly been growing in me since God called me to the Song of Solomon.

GOD'S FIERY EMOTIONS

UNDERSTANDING GOD'S DESIRE for human beings is very important now because His judgments are about to be loosed across the globe, for the passion of God's love and the fire of His vengeance are one emotion. This consuming fire—His pleasure, His desire, His burning love—will burn up all that hinders love. His burning holiness is an expression of His fiery love. In Exodus 20:5, God adds another dimension and says:

> For I, the LORD your God, am a jealous God.

The focus of His pleasure is toward human beings, and He is jealous over them with hot, fiery emotion.

The emotions of God strike terror. In this passage, we are not only terrified by the pressure of judgment, but we are terrified and awestruck by the grandeur of the holy romance. It is terrifying to encounter a God like this. It makes no sense and seems outrageous in the most holy way—the glory of being embraced, adorned and enthroned even though we were formerly rebels. This is the logic of the gospel. It is the outflow of the burning heart of the uncreated God.

Approximately five hundred years after the time of Moses,

David came along and saw this burning God, this God of pleasure. David developed a theology of holy pleasure, and therefore he addresses the beauty of God and how this beauty is imparted to the redeemed.

Psalm 36:8 is one of my favorite verses. Here David talks about drinking from the river of God's pleasure—touching the very being of God. David understood that God is a fountain of passionate spiritual desire, and he was tapping into it.

> They are abundantly satisfied with the fullness of Your
>   house,
> And You give them drink from the river of Your pleasures.
> For with You is the fountain of life;
> In Your light we see light.
>
> —PSALM 36:8-9

He also touches on the subject of holy lovesickness. David has this unquenchable longing, and nothing can satisfy him. No military victory or earthly experience in the human arena can satisfy the depths of his longing for God. David comes forth as one of the first theologians of holy romance.

In Psalm 16, David articulates the theology of God's pleasure for His people that burns in His heart and the pleasure that He imparts to people in His embrace.

> You will show me the path of life;
> In Your presence is fullness of joy:
> At Your right hand are pleasures forevermore.
>
> —PSALM 16:11

Today's weary church needs a vision of the pleasure of seeing His beauty. We need a vision of the holy romance that will empower us to meet the End-Time challenges of both the judgment and harvest.

The Scriptures describe the divine river of fiery passion. The prophet Daniel, who came on the scene five hundred years after David, speaks about the same river David spoke of, but he uses different language. In Daniel 7:10, he calls it a river of burning fire that proceeds out of the throne of God.

> A river of fire was flowing, coming out from before him. Thousands upon thousands attended him; ten thousand times ten thousand stood before him. The court was seated, and the books were opened.
>
> NIV

Daniel saw a river of fire coming out of the throne of God. It was God Himself in burning desire and lovesickness. God will destroy everything that hinders love. His Son desired a partner, so the Father longed to give a companion to Him. This uncreated river of fire is flowing out of the throne, and God Himself is its only source. When he saw this river, I believe that Daniel saw God the Holy Spirit.

A River of Fire

ANOTHER FIVE HUNDRED years after Daniel saw that incredible vision of the river of God, the apostle John arrived on the scene. In Acts 2:3, when one hundred twenty intercessors were praying in the upper room, the fire broke out into the natural realm, appearing as flames above each person's head.

> When the Day of Pentecost had fully come, they were all with one accord in one place. And suddenly there came a sound from heaven, as of a rushing mighty wind, and it

71

> filled the whole house where they were sitting. Then there appeared to them divided tongues, as of fire, and one sat upon each of them. And they were all filled with the Holy Spirit and began to speak with other tongues, as the Spirit gave them utterance.
>
> —ACTS 2:1–4

Everyone saw the fire that day, and it rested on each of them. Even though this fire barely touched them, it energized them and made them people from another world. This river of fire consumes what is bad and transforms sinful men into people who are delightful to God. When the river touched those intercessors in the upper room, it turned men and women who were weak and cowardly into people from another realm.

Such men and women walk in the reality of the age to come. Carnal pleasures such as money and other earthly desires will be seen in an entirely different perspective. Now that the river of fire has touched them, these people redefine reward, success and pleasure. They feel differently about everything. They will still be humans, and therefore they will continue to struggle with sin and weakness occasionally. But although their human struggles have not been removed as they will be in the final resurrection, a drastic change has taken place. These individuals will never again be the same.

John was one of those who was touched in the upper room on the Day of Pentecost. He was touched by the fire that Daniel talked about. He experienced the river of pleasure that David spoke of and wanted to drink from and swim in. In Revelation 15 John goes beyond the descriptions of Daniel and David when he tells us about the sea of fire. In this passage the river of God overflows into the sea of fire!

All the saints at the end, the bride on the last day, are on that vast sea before the throne, mingled in flaming fire.

> And I saw something like a sea of glass mingled with fire, and those who have the victory over the beast, over his image and over his mark and over the number of his name, standing on the sea of glass, having harps of God.
> —REVELATION 15:2

Seeking pleasure is a primary pursuit of individuals today. But where does deep, lasting and superior pleasure come from, and how can it be found? The answer is actually very simple. It comes the throne of God, from God Himself, and it's found in the river of His fire. It's found in God's burning desire and passion for you. When you experience the answer yourself, when you discover the deep, lasting and superior pleasure of that river, its delightful waters will sustain you through absolutely anything. Then when the world is colliding with all of the judgments of God, the great harvest and the victorious church, your heart will be supernaturally buoyed up with power. But if you neglect to become immersed in the river of fire, God will still bring His entire church into the stability of experiencing His pleasures, but you will be left unprepared for the wild ride of the last generation. This wild ride of glory and of pain will be unprecedented in human history.

THE BRIDEGROOM GENERATION

SOMETHING IS ON the horizon for Planet Earth for which the church is completely unprepared. An unprepared church cannot possibly prepare an unprepared world.

Evolutionists reject the fact that God created the earth, and they believe that intelligence, training and education will cause conditions for the human race to get better and better. They are completely unaware that Someone is going to confront Planet Earth. Therefore, it is wise, excellent and necessary to be totally given to God right now.

That Someone who is coming is not a comet. He who is coming measures the universe with the span of His hand. Beloved, He is coming in fierceness to terrify the nations. (See Revelation 19.) No evolutionary philosophy, no technology of man, no training or education will stop His judgments. My friend, the world is completely unprepared for what lies ahead. The day of the Lord is a day of fire. (See 2 Peter 3:7.) And a Bridegroom who is a consuming fire will burn passionately with both love and judgment.

God's mercy to the globe is a prepared church, a prepared bride. She will be prepared because she will be empowered by holy romance with her Bridegroom God. From her sense of spiritual romance, she will view everything differently. She will know the greatest pleasure that comes when God reveals God to the human spirit. Because this bride is lost in the spiritual pleasure and the delight of lovesickness, she will interpret the events of the last days through a lens of love. As God's temporal judgments disrupt the human race, the End-Time bride will see God's hand of mercy in them. Those people who make up the bride of Christ will find their greatest pleasure in God. They will find their glory in the resurrection, not in great buildings. They will live as people from a different world, a people lost in the passion of holy romance.

Currently the Western church is focused on things of this world and not on the Bridegroom, Jesus Christ. Because Christians today are still deeply rooted and grounded in this world, we are woefully unprepared to be the agents of grace that the human race needs to prepare it for what is ahead. God is beckoning the human race. Now is the time for the people of God to press into Him and to enter into divine romance. Without this, we will be completely unprepared.

The theology of the holy romance must be laid down for believers. Many people have a *yes* in their spirits, but too many are leaving the exploration of this theology to someone else. However, this theology must be worked through by today's believers, by you and by me, and not by someone else.

The subject of pursuing and experiencing spiritual pleasure is vast, and it has many tensions and paradoxes. Moving into the depths of the Spirit will cause an individual to give up many worldly pleasures to experience spiritual ones. Jesus told only the new beginners to count the cost. But counting the cost only happens on the front end. On the back end, as Paul reflected back on his sacrifices for God, he says he gave up nothing but rubbish. He may have given up a brilliant career and money, but he counted such things as garbage.

> Yet indeed I also count all things loss for the excellence of the knowledge of Christ Jesus my Lord, for whom I have suffered the loss of all things, and count them as rubbish, that I may gain Christ.
>
> —PHILIPPIANS 3:8

By his own description, Paul's life as a follower of Christ was filled with hardship:

> In labors more abundant, in stripes above measure, in prisons more frequently, in deaths often. From the Jews five times I received forty stripes minus one. Three times I was beaten with rods; once I was stoned; three times I was shipwrecked; a night and a day I have been in the

deep; in journeys often, in perils of waters, in perils of robbers, in perils of my own countrymen, in perils of the Gentiles, in perils in the city, in perils in the wilderness, in perils in the sea, in perils among false brethren; in weariness and toil, in sleeplessness often, in hunger and thirst, in fastings often, in cold and nakedness—besides the other things, what comes upon me daily: my deep concern for all the churches.

—2 CORINTHIANS 11:23–28

Amazingly, Paul counted such difficulties as but "momentary light affliction," all so that he could win Christ. (See 2 Corinthians 4:17, NAS.)

As the birth pangs of End-Time events raise the heat of affliction in the lives of both believers and unbelievers, divine pleasures of love and supernatural security will make the yoke of such difficulties much easier to wear. Believers will agree with the apostle that such difficulties are but momentary light afflictions, unworthy to be compared to the glory that is to come.

Nevertheless, great bitterness and fear will tempt those who do not enter into the superior pleasure—into the holy romance of the gospel. These people will become very confused, for many things that will occur will only make sense in the context of the experience of holy romance.

DIVINE AND WORLDLY PLEASURES

WHEN WE EXPERIENCE and discover the ways of superior pleasures, we redefine reward, success and pleasure. We live as people from another world because that's precisely what we are. The world has the wrong answer for how to experience pleasure. Its answer is inferior; worldly pleasures cannot truly satisfy us. The pleasures of the world leave us painfully craving for more. History and religion have taught the church that it is wrong to experience any kind of pleasure. They tell the church to grit her teeth, try harder and endure. But when the church complies, she only becomes molded into religious self-determination.

The true gospel brings people into the *romance* of God. This is a term that I use, and I believe it's permissible to use it although it is not a biblical term. The word *trinity* is also not a biblical term, but it is certainly a biblical concept.

I call this generation the "Bridegroom generation" because I believe that the realities of the Bridegroom will be uniquely manifested in the very last generation. The church's revelation of the Bridegroom will far surpass the degree of revelation she has received throughout her history. This revelation will include the beauty of the Lord, which will be seen in great measure, the identity of the bride and the power to walk in the first commandment and therefore in the second commandment.

It's time for the church to receive her vision for the holy romance. Why not invest the next five to ten years of your own life to pursue this with abandonment? Throw your being into the pursuit of holy romance with the Bridegroom. Let a vision for holy romance become your first priority. Establish your own personal vision for the first commandment so that you focus your life on it, and you will find that the power to fulfill it will be completely supplied by God. The generation the Lord returns is what I refer to as the Bridegroom generation. This generation of God's people— the Bridegroom generation—will experience unprecedented revelation and power.

We must proclaim this message of spiritual romance

with boldness. We must call the multitudes to enter into the romance of the Bridegroom. For when they do, they will be able to make sense of the King with His harvest and the Judge who terrifies nations. The harvest and the judgments will not make sense without a revelation of the Bridegroom's love and beauty. We must give people courage to seek and believe that they can experience the depths of God's presence. We must look at our own despair and weakness and throw it off in the light of God's Word, and we must dare to believe God with courage in this exciting generation.

THE DISRUPTION OF THE LOVESICK

LOVESICK, CAPTURED PEOPLE live differently. This holy lovesickness is serious, and its implications will create a massive disruption wherever the lovesick bride goes.

Your lovesickness for the Bridegroom and your identity as the bride will drive you into activities that will enrage others. You will disturb the status quo. You will threaten religion. Why? Because lovesick people cannot be bribed or bought off. They are not driven by a political spirit, and therefore they are not afraid of losing anything.

Lovesick people have no price tags. You cannot control people who have no fear. In fact, you could offer them their pick of all the political positions in society and in the church world, and they would remain unmoved.

One part of the globe will follow them because nothing is more attractive than a heart on fire for the Son of God. Unsaved multitudes will come into the harvest when they see lovesickness burning brightly in human beings. The people to be harvested will at first look at the church and say, "We want something to die for!" As a lovesick contingency emerges worldwide, those who are on fire for the Son of God will bring in the harvest, and the explosive power of this ingathering of souls will awaken the church. The fire they see in us will draw a portion of the world's people, and they will love it. They will be intrigued, mystified and wooed by it. They will follow it and give themselves to it. They will become lovesick themselves.

Another part of the globe will be confused, and these individuals will start controversies. Many will name the name of Jesus. They will do anything they can to undermine the holy passion that will sweep the church and the world, and they will come up with any theology they can find to put it down and silence it.

Others will become so enraged that they will kill believers. Martyrdom will be an increasing issue as we draw closer to the end. The nations will be enraged by this fiery love for the Bridegroom. This is going to cause trouble. Glory and trouble are both coming.

Violent Love

LOVE WILL MAKE you spiritually violent for the kingdom of God—violent enough to endure persecution and even martyrdom. The Bible says the violent will take the kingdom by force.

> And from the days of John the Baptist until now the kingdom of heaven suffers violence, and the violent take it by force.
>
> —MATTHEW 11:12

A holy violent love will make us live very differently before

God. This passion of love that is so strong as to be violent will keep you from ever quitting or giving up. Let your heart be molded into the heart of a lovesick bride and become an individual such as John who rested his head upon the heart of God.

Become like Mary of Bethany. Become a man or woman with Mary's heart of adoration, love and worship.

THE ALABASTER BOX ANOINTING

And when Jesus was in Bethany at the house of Simon the leper, a woman came to Him having an alabaster flask of very costly fragrant oil, and she poured it on His head as He sat at the table. But when His disciples saw it, they were indignant, saying, "Why this waste? For this fragrant oil might have been sold for much and given to the poor."

But when Jesus was aware of it, He said to them, "Why do you trouble the woman? For she has done a good work for Me. For you have the poor with you always, but Me you do not have always. For in pouring this fragrant oil on My body, she did it for My burial. Assuredly, I say to you, wherever this gospel is preached in the whole world, what this woman has done will also be told as a memorial to her."

—MATTHEW 26:6-13

I really like the heart of Mary of Bethany. She was not an apostle. She was never famous, never wrote a book, never did a conference and never said much. Her passionate love was in secret—she just loved the Lord ferociously in secret. She took all she had, her earthly treasure—an alabaster box filled with spikenard, worth thirty thousand dollars—and she lavishly, extravagantly poured it upon the One she loved.

All the apostles were mad, not just Judas. In fact, everyone was mad about this. But Jesus ignored their reactions. He silenced their accusations by honoring this adoring worshiper. Jesus knew that she would never write a book or speak at a conference or do anything of worldly significance, but despite her obscurity, no one would ever forget how she moved the heart of Christ with her love.

Something magnificent happens when human beings recognize the gold of the pleasure of this romance and choose it instead of the sawdust of this world. Something amazing happens when we look at God and see His incredible worth. Something superb happens when we fall in love with Him and put our own gold in the dust.

> If you return to the Almighty, you will be built up; you will remove iniquity far from your tents. Then you will lay your gold in the dust, and the gold of Ophir among the stones of the brooks. Yes, the Almighty will be your gold and your precious silver; for then you will have your delight in the Almighty, and lift up your face to God.
> —Job 22:23-26

In His mercy, God will reward forever those who consider Him gold—who are overwhelmed by the precious Savior's unfathomable value. God just looks for ways to bless us. He honors us so much more greatly than our simple responses to Him deserve. He honors us disproportionately and beyond measure just because we choose Him over the sin that will result in our judgment. It is unbelievable that He responds in this way just because we see who He is.

Personally, I am going to grab hold of this holy invitation. It doesn't seem fair that Christ rewards me beyond measure just because I said no to sawdust and caught the revelation of a little bit of the truth about who He is. But He likes when we choose Him—He really likes it. Our decision to see His worth simply delights His heart.

Jesus cries out to us:

> Set me as a seal upon your heart,
> As a seal upon your arm;
> For love is as strong as death,
> Jealousy as cruel as the grave;
> Its flames are flames of fire,
> A most vehement flame.
> Many waters cannot quench love,
> Nor can the floods drown it.
> If a man would give for love all the wealth of his house,
> It would be utterly despised.
>
> —SONG OF SOLOMON 8:6–7

I pray for the seal of Song of Solomon 8:6–7 to be upon you. I pray that seal of His love that is as strong as death will be placed upon your heart! The vehement flames of God's love are unquenchable and cannot be drowned. With this divine seal upon us, everything else will seem as but dung so that we might experience more of Christ.

The Lord will put a seal of fire over the hearts of His people. He will do this all over the earth.

> *O Lord, let the burning heart of the uncreated God touch us! Let us swim in it; let us get lost in it. Let it make us people of another age—let us burn like bright righteousness so that unbelievers will come in by the multitudes. Give us passion, O Lord.*

Give us courage to stand for the holy romance, for the beauty and the pleasures of the bride and the Bridegroom. Give us the power to seek it. It takes God to love God. Burning and jealous God, come and burn in us!

THIS IS MY BELOVED AND THIS IS MY FRIEND,
O DAUGHTERS OF JERUSALEM.

—SONG OF SOLOMON 5:16, NAS

5

The Bride's
Portrait of Jesus

With her heart spilling over with supernatural tenderness, the bride of Christ gazes upon the holy majesty of her heavenly Bridegroom. From the intimacy of the secret chambers of her heart, out of the depths of love and magnificent devotion, an exalted, heavenly song flows forth. The Song of Solomon is a description of the Bridegroom through the eyes of a lovesick bride.

So powerful are the words that flow supernaturally from her lips that understanding the parables she recites will strengthen your heart with power to persevere through even the fiercest storm. To understand the heart of the lovesick bride in these passages is to see God in a depth that few of us are privileged to enter. As together we behold our Bridegroom through the Shulamite's eyes, I pray that God will open the eyes of your understanding and illuminate your heart to one of the greatest mysteries of our wonderful faith.

PERSEVERING LOVE

THE SECRET OF the bride's persevering love for Jesus while in the midst of trials is described in poetic language in Song of Solomon 5:10–16:

> My beloved is white [radiant] and ruddy,
> Chief among ten thousand.
> His head is like the finest gold;
> His locks are wavy,
> And black as a raven.
> His eyes are like doves
> By the rivers of waters,
> Washed with milk,
> And fitly set.
> His cheeks are like a bed of spices,
> Banks of scented herbs.
> His lips are lilies,
> Dripping liquid myrrh.
> His hands are rods of gold
> Set with beryl.
> His body is carved ivory
> Inlaid with sapphires.
> His legs are pillars of marble
> Set on bases of fine gold.
> His countenance is like Lebanon,
> Excellent as the cedars.
> His mouth is most sweet,
> Yes, he is altogether lovely.
> This is my beloved,
> And this is my friend,
> O daughters of Jerusalem!

Here, as she is tested, the young bride gives one of the most powerful descriptions of Jesus. This passage is one of the most outstanding expressions of worship in the Word of God. This is the one time in the song in which she pours herself out in worship to the King. Admittedly, you may not quickly feel the power of this passage. It is a magnificent, poetic unveiling of the splendor of Christ Jesus and an outstanding statement of her love.

This passage is written in poetic language that allows us to reach new depths of understanding, and it is meant to equip our souls to effectively worship God in our own time of trial. This passage is a must for us to master as we grow in mature bridal affections for Jesus. This is not a passage that we can read and understand without deep meditation. Read these verses over and over and search out the depth.

The Holy Spirit speaks in poetic parables to provide multiple layers of rich understanding for the hungry soul. God often speaks of deep things in the hidden language so that the spiritual hungry will seek out deeper meaning. Christ taught parables for two reasons: to make truth easy and to make truth difficult so that only the hungry heart of love could experience them.

The Song of Solomon is a love song; therefore, Solomon writes in the poetic language of love, providing endless depths to enjoy.

TEN ATTRIBUTES OF GOD

WHICH ONE OF us doesn't long to see God? We can do so right now through the eyes of the Shulamite. When she beheld her beloved, she described him beautifully and powerfully so that we might behold him also. In this passage, the Holy

Spirit uses metaphors of the human body to convey ten attributes of God. We can use Scripture to interpret Scripture as a guide for this parabolic language. The Shulamite gives a very poetic and dynamic statement of the glory of Jesus using twelve descriptive statements of Jesus. The first one is a general statement. The ten distinct attributes of God are then described, and the last statement is a summary.

The bride describes Jesus by using the imagery of the temple, combining it with imagery of the human body. The Holy Spirit is depicting the majesty of Jesus Christ in the language of the temple with gold, precious stones, ivory and the cedars of Lebanon. Why? These were symbols that people of her day would have been familiar with.

The Holy Spirit uses these metaphors in other parts of Scripture so that we can interpret them according to His intention. Remember that the Holy Spirit is describing the beauty of Christ's personality, not His physical features. The passage as a whole is written to show the excellency of Jesus as being "above all other beloved." (See Song of Solomon 5:9.) The bride depicts ten attributes of Jesus, each of which has two descriptions. It is not possible to fully develop any of these ten attributes. They contain great depths of meaning. My only purpose here is to offer a mere seed of understanding that you may water over the years through long and loving meditation on this passage.

You can grow in your understanding of these ten attributes and effectively meditate on God's beauty by speaking these truths back to God in worship and prayer. I encourage you to try this. These wonderful words have the power to transport our hearts into the glorious realm of intimacy for which our heart deeply longs.

In this particular portion of the Song of Solomon, the bride has been severely tested. I call it the ultimate twofold test. Such seasons of testing are common to all who go deep in the Lord.

Here one less mature part of the body of Christ asks the bride a deep question seeking to learn the secret to her persevering love in the midst of deep trials.

The Shulamite answers by saying, "My beloved is white [radiant] and ruddy" (Song of Sol. 5:10).

I like the phrase *my beloved* because it shows that she maintains her affection for Jesus through her present season of testing. She harbors no resentment in her heart toward Jesus. She is not offended by her trial and does not stumble. He is still her beloved. There are times after a hard season that our burning desire diminishes a little, and we no longer call Him *my beloved.* Instead we say, "My heart is hurt. I don't trust You. My spirit is wounded. I've closed my heart off from You because You keep mistreating me by allowing these trials to come into my life."

Negativity can flow out of our spirits during these times of testing. The goal, however, is that in the midst of trials we open our spirits with affection, trusting His leadership without beginning to guard our hearts in fear of more hurt. When this happens, our woundedness affects our relationship with God, and our intimacy with Jesus can be hindered. Harboring offense in our hearts toward God wounds our love for Him, and the devil knows this very well.

He Is Radiant

IN THE GENERAL description she cries out that "He is white" (Song of Sol. 5:10). The New International Version reads, "He is radiant." The New American Standard says, "He is dazzling."

The Hebrew word translated as "white" means either "radiant," "dazzling," "brilliant" or "shining white." The idea is that Jesus is stunning and dazzling to His bride. He is "brilliant in His loveliness" and "radiant in His splendor," abounding with unapproachable light that dwells around His throne. (See 1 Timothy 6:16, NAS.) She proclaims the dazzling splendor of God's Person. The dazzling brilliance that surrounds the resurrected Christ's Person is made up of all the bright colors, shining lights, exotic fragrances, awesome power, heavenly sounds and beautiful music. The resurrected Christ possesses indescribable beauty and splendor.

The house of an interior decorator has a certain excellence and symmetry. Every color is set in proper contrast to all the other colors. God is the ultimate interior decorator, and His throne is the ultimate place of excellence. The ambiance around God's throne is incredible. His city is dazzling like a perfect celestial diamond shining with brilliance.

Revelation 4:3 describes the Father's throne as being like a sardius and a jasper stone.

> And He who was sitting was like a jasper stone and a sardius in appearance; and there was a rainbow around the throne, like an emerald in appearance.
>
> —NAS

The ancient jasper stone was like a transparent diamond-like gem, and a sardius is a deep red gem. An emerald rainbow also encircles the throne. The brilliantly fantastic colors associated with the person of God and Jesus' fragrances are real, not just metaphors. (See 2 Corinthians 2:15.)

The throne of God is drenched in His lovely fragrances, and these awesome fragrances fill the entire eternal city.

The power of God's energy releases an invisible but

discernible feeling of His manifest presence. God's discernible power flows from His Throne.

The sounds around the throne of God are also majestic and wonderful. They include the sound of musical instruments and voices, as well as thunder, the sound of many waters, citywide applause with prophetic proclamations, choruses and mighty winds.

> And from the throne proceeded lightnings, thunderings, and voices.
>
> —REVELATION 4:5

Thunder, lightning, voices and sounds come out of the throne of God. They are probably as terrifying as they are sweet and beautiful. Such descriptions are associated with the idea of Jesus being dazzling and stunning. We can experience the presence of God through powerful spiritual senses. Think of the kind of energy we will feel in the very court of God!

HE IS RUDDY

THE BRIDE GOES on to add that Jesus is ruddy. Ruddy suggests that He had a red complexion. It's even said of King David that his appearance was ruddy, with reddish hair and a reddish complexion. His ruddiness caused him to stand out from all the other Jewish boys in Israel at that time who more typically had darker hair and a darker complexion. The symbolism of ruddy refers to Jesus' having a good and fresh complexion, for when one's complexion is ruddy, it's considered healthy.

Ruddiness speaks of all the signs of health, youth, vigor, maturity and beauty. Altogether, His attributes are lovely. With adoring eyes of supernatural love, the bride beholds His perfection and cries, "He's altogether lovely. His is perfection.

Nothing in Him is marred; He has no blemish. This is my Beloved—He is utter perfection."

She also is saying that He possesses a wholesome and perfect balance in all of His attributes. In other words, He is healthy in all His attributes. They are perfectly balanced. This statement holds more than the sense that Jesus has perfect balance in all of His noble characteristics, such as perfect mercy and perfect judgment. He is not ruddy because of the perfect unity of all His characteristics, but He is balanced because He lacks nothing. He is 100 percent of each of His attributes: He is 100 percent eternally, infinitely righteous and 100 percent eternally and infinitely merciful. It is not His unity of parts, but His sheer absence of parts.

Another perspective of symbols of *white* and the *ruddy* mean this: The *white* speaks of Christ's divine nature—He is fully God. The *ruddy* speaks of His human nature and refers to the blood. As a human high priest, He offered up His own blood, so He is fully God and fully man. His glory is so unique that it unites both attributes. He is the only One in heaven or on earth who has, at the same time, the fullness of humanity and the fullness of deity. God the Father and the angels are not like that. Christ is completely unique in His own category.

His unique beauty springs forth from the balance of two opposing elements. He is both the lion and the lamb at the exact same time, and He perfectly expresses both elements in His personality without contradiction. The lion roars with boldness, and the lamb submits with meekness. He is both, and He yields His heart to His bride. He is actually interested in the things that are in your heart!

CHIEF AMONG TEN THOUSAND

HE IS CHIEF among ten thousand. The phrase *ten thousand*

refers to an incomparably great number. The number is not meant to be taken literally, but indicates an extremely large number. God has given Christ preeminence above everybody and everything. The word *chief* literally means that "He is lifted up as a banner among a large number," or that "He would be distinguished as a banner among a multitude." He is the *chief,* which in Hebrew means "the banner that distinguishes Him among all the multitudes." For example, in a great parade where every banner looked the same, one distinct banner would attract the attention of all the masses. He is worthy because He is unique and distinct in His beauty.

Throughout the rest of this description the bride uses the imagery of the temple. Of course, Solomon, who wrote this love song, is the one who built the great Jewish temple, which was one of the greatest buildings on earth at that time in history.

Now that we are finished glancing at the bride's general description of the beauty of God, let us take a look at ten specific attributes of the Bridegroom.

LIKE FINEST GOLD

THE FIRST ATTRIBUTE is in Song of Solomon 5:11. *His head is like the finest gold.* I do not believe that the bride is trying to describe Him in the natural. Instead, spiritual language, or the language of the temple, is being used. In this imagery, the Holy Spirit depicts the majesty and the divine excellence of Jesus Christ. The head, the most prominent part of the body, sets the direction for the rest of the body. The head speaks partially of Jesus' leadership over the church.

Another passage of Scripture, 1 Corinthians 11:3, says that the head of Christ is God, so the head may also speak of the

Trinity—the Father, the Son and the Holy Spirit—the triune God existing in perfect affection and unity. The head can speak of the Father's leadership over all.

Christ's head speaks of Jesus' sovereignty as well as being a picture of His Father's sovereignty. In other words, the head of Jesus symbolizes Christ's sovereignty and His relationship of the Trinity, too.

Our heavenly Bridegroom's head, or leadership, *is like the finest gold*. Gold is bright, solid and the most precious of all building materials. It suggests the highest degree of quality and excellence imaginable to the human mind. The finest gold has no impurities—and Christ in His sovereignty has no impurities at all.

Gold typically speaks of deity, but when the bride extravagantly tells about Christ's leadership, she says He's the finest of the finest gold. He is the most pure and most precious possible.

I'm sure that you have heard the phrase that total power corrupts totally. This statement is true in the human arena, but total authority does not corrupt Jesus Christ. His head is finest gold and cannot be improved upon. There is nothing that can be added to the leadership of Jesus Christ over His church.

Interestingly, in His leadership Jesus never suspends one attribute to exercise another. When He is kind, He never violates His holiness. When He is holy, He never undermines kindness. His head, His leadership, is the finest gold and can never be improved upon. This truth comforts us under trials and helps us to look toward Him instead of believing the lies of the devil, which seek to confuse us and make us think that God is like the devil and the devil is like God.

When times are tough, come to God and tell Him, "Your head is the finest gold." Speaking that one sentence is like honey to your spirit as the Spirit of the Lord touches your heart.

His Hair

NEXT, THE PASSAGE says that *His locks are wavy and black as a raven.* His locks are His hair, which refers to His commitment and dedication to God and to people. Samson and the prophet Samuel both made vows that they would not cut their hair. In the Book of Judges when Samson broke that vow and cut his hair, it indicated that he had violated the commitment he made to God. Thus it is common to see the long hair of the Nazirite vow to speak of dedication.

This reference to hair can have other meanings as well. Christ is perfectly dedicated to God. However, His dedication is more than just to God; He is dedicated to us as well.

The New International Version describes His hair as *wavy.* But the King James Version calls it *bushy.* Jesus' hair is thick and wavy. It is the hair of a young man in the prime of life as contrasted to an old man whose hair has lost its fullness and vitality. Baldness is the opposite of wavy hair. This suggests that Christ's dedication to us if full of vigor. Jesus is not at the end of the race and losing strength to love us.

The description of Christ's hair is that it is *black as a raven.* His hair is not only wavy, but black as a raven. The raven speaks of pure black, and His hair speaks of His youthful, energetic zeal. Black hair is in contrast to the gray hair of old men. His hair is youthful. It proves that Jesus is not at the end of His resources to love, but His affection possesses full strength and vigor.

The message here is that Christ's consecration to God and to His people is eternally vigorous. Some people say they have been serving God so long that they are worn out. What they are saying is that their dedication is becoming as hair that is gray and balding. Jesus' dedication, on the other hand, never grows old, tired and weary. His bride is wonderfully secure because she has no reason to fear that His dedication will grow old, get sick or die. He is forever in His prime and at the highest peak of His love, passion and dedication.

God has no moods. His hair is always wavy and black. Therefore, we never have to be concerned as to whether it is a good time to approach Him.

HIS EYES

THE THIRD ATTRIBUTE of the Bridegroom is that *His eyes are like doves.* She goes on to add that they are like doves *by the rivers of water washed with milk and fitly set.* Christ sees all things, so His eyes suggest His omniscience, which means "all knowledge." His eyes also refer to His ability to see or to His discernment.

> And there is no creature hidden from His sight, but all things are naked and open to the eyes of Him to whom we must give account.
> —HEBREWS 4:13

Even those things that are hidden in darkness are completely clear to the Lord because He sees both the good and the bad. Most people think of God as only seeing the negative. They say that God knows their bad stuff, which is true, but that is where His mercy comes in. When you understand that He thoroughly knows your bad stuff, then the blood of Jesus is more precious than ever. It doesn't make you draw away from God but makes you praise Him.

He also sees the good qualities in your life and the willingness in your spirit—even more than you can see them yourself. We try to obey God but stumble outwardly. By doing this, we mirror what Samuel did when he was anointing David;

we look at the outward appearance. When we stumble, we feel as if we are total hypocrites, and then we want to quit. God sees us fall, but He also sees the cry in our hearts to obey Him and succeed. Many times this truth has given me the courage to go on.

Because God sees your private longings for righteousness, He also acknowledges the finances that you sow secretly into His kingdom. He sees the prayer and the times when you did well but were slandered for it. God even sees things that are hidden from the eyes of man, and He rewards you for them.

> Therefore judge nothing before the time, until the Lord comes, who will both bring to light the hidden things of darkness and reveal the counsels of the hearts. Then each one's praise will come from God.
>
> —1 CORINTHIANS 4:5

Don't even attempt to perfectly judge your own heart right now, because you cannot even fully see yourself. On the last day, God will grant you praise for the things that He sees about you that you do not even realize are true about yourself. He is the only One with perfect sight.

No one understands as God does. People say that they have yet to meet somebody who understands them and realizes what they've gone through. But Jesus' eyes see what you've been through, what you're dealing with now and what you'll face in the future. He knows how you've stood under unbelievable pressures of life.

> For God is not unjust to forget your work and labor of love which you have shown toward His name, in that you have ministered to the saints, and do minister.
>
> —HEBREWS 6:10

97

God will reward you for the good deeds that you have done, for His eyes have seen everyone. When we receive this revelation of His eyes, we no longer feel compelled to rehearse our glory stories so often. We don't have to prove things that have already been proven in His sight. King David is a prime example of a person who possessed this unique ability or the grace of God to understand how God saw him.

His eyes are like doves. This attribute speaks of singleness of vision and purity. A dove cannot look in two places; it does not possess peripheral vision. It can only see straight ahead. In addition, doves speak of purity and of the Holy Spirit.

Next, His eyes are like doves *by the rivers of water.* The waters are where the doves bathe themselves and become clean. So not only are Jesus' eyes all seeing, but they are clean. The way in which He interprets knowledge is through a clean heart.

For example, you may stand before a judge with a true story, but if that judge has an unclean heart, he will misinterpret your heart. His ability to see your heart will be limited by his own jaded perspective because of the sin resident within his heart. On the other hand, Jesus' eyes are clean like a dove's, which are bathed by the rivers washed with milk. Discernment and interpretation of what He sees is not like that of a fallen, wounded, dysfunctional and sinful judge who is limited by the darkness in his own soul. Christ's eyes possess purity and innocence like that of doves who are bathed and cleaned. There is no distortion in the interpretation of the facts that He sees.

WASHED WITH MILK

HIS EYES ARE by the rivers of waters *washed with milk.* Obviously, there is no such thing as rivers that have milk in them, so a spiritual point is being made here. Christ's eyes are pure, white and clean, and they speak of the purity of His discernment. Milk is the simplicity and innocence of His childlikeness. Jesus is not childish, but He is both infinitely complex and simple at the same time. He is a divine paradox, the lion and the lamb, the childlike and the complex. That extreme opposites exist within the personality of one divine being is beyond our ability to understand.

His eyes are also *fitly set*. This comparison is like that of a jewel that is fitly set by the most skillful artist when constructing a very expensive piece of jewelry. The artist will take a diamond and skillfully set it into a bracelet or necklace.

That His eyes are fitly set means there is not deformity in them. In other words, His eyes are not too deep, nor do they protrude in an unlovely way. His discernment is perfect, for He sees and judges every situation without exaggeration or deformity. His vision and knowledge are perfect, being neither farsighted nor nearsighted. He knows all the strategies of the enemy, but He also understands those things that are important and precious to your life.

Psalm 139:1-18 says that God knows everything that is important to your heart. The Lord is aware of the things that are important to your heart, and He will give them to you later when it serves the purposes of God in your life. You will receive some of the things that are important to you in the age to come, not in this age.

His Cheeks

THIS PORTION OF Scripture continues, *His cheeks are like a bed of spices, banks of scented herbs.* Cheeks express the countenance of one's face because the cheeks are windows to the emotions, enabling others to know whether a person is joyful, sad or angry. A person's cheeks can tell you what kind of mood he or she is in. The cheeks reveal the internal emotional state and reveal the inner beauty of the countenance.

Christ's cheeks are like *a bed of spices,* which points to the diversity of His passion, pleasures and delights. It's like a garden of beautiful, fragrant spices. They express His emotions that are diverse, beautiful and give wide range to pleasure and delight.

The song says that Jesus' cheeks are also like *banks of scented herbs.* This speaks of the extravagant fragrance and diversity of His affections. Sweet-smelling flowers in full blossom suggest a most delightful garden. That is the emotional makeup of Jesus Christ—His passion for you, His longing for you and His delight in you. It is also the Father's delight over His Son, the Son's delight over His Father and the Father's passion and pleasure over His creation. Jesus also delights over the increase of His kingdom and His holiness.

HIS LIPS

VERSE 13 PROVIDES more description by telling us, *His lips are lilies, dripping liquid myrrh.* Lips speak of His Word, and His mouth speaks of His communication and intimacy. This portrayal refers to the power of His Word.

His words are like two things: They are like *lilies,* and they are *dripping liquid myrrh.* Lilies are sweet and satisfying. Psalm 19:10 says God's words are "sweeter also than honey and the honeycomb." When our heart's desire is to obey Him, His Word is sweet and satisfying. The Bible comes alive when the heart's intent is to obey Him 100 percent. That's when the Word becomes sweet. Deliberate resistance to God's Word makes it seem dull and dead to your heart. It loses its sweetness and no longer satisfies as the lilies, which are fragrant, innocent and tender.

Jesus' words are also compared to *dripping liquid myrrh.* He does not just give us the sweet, refreshing affirmation and fragrance of the lilies but also myrrh, which involves suffering. Myrrh and frankincense were used as burial spices. The fragrance comes as we embrace death to the flesh so that we might find resurrection in the grace of God. His words have the fragrance of the lilies, but they also drip with myrrh. Jesus knows how to give tough love and correction. He not only tells you that things are good, but as a loving Father, He also tells you when to stop and how to change.

Hebrews 12:5–6 says:

> My son, do not despise the chastening of the LORD, nor be discouraged when you are rebuked by Him; for whom the LORD loves He chastens.

The words of correction that God gives us bring life. His Word challenges us to die to ourselves in a greater way so that we can be a more mature member of the bride of Christ.

In Malachi 2:17, the Lord told the people of Israel that their words wearied Him because they said individuals who did evil were good. These people called evil things good and good things evil. The words of God's people are sometimes too affirming. Too often we refuse to call something impure when that's exactly what it is. Some of us just do not possess the ability to speak words that have myrrh in them; we can only speak words that have lilies. We need to discern between good and evil, as God has done in His Word.

HIS HANDS

THE NEXT VERSE says, *His hands are rods of gold set with beryl.* His hands or arms refer to the way that He accomplishes His work. This speaks of His perfect power, omnipotence and sovereign activity. It also refers to His ability to accomplish anything that He pleases, both in the natural creation and in the spiritual realm. He accomplished your redemption and reigns over all His works throughout the eternal ages. His hands are skillful in accomplishing everything that is good, and they are like gold. All that He does has godly purity behind it, for everything He does is filled with wisdom, love and divine power.

HIS BODY

HIS BODY IS carved ivory inlaid with sapphires. In the King James Version, Christ's body is called His belly. It is the Hebrew idea of tender compassion. They would have said that out of their bellies flowed tender compassion. This speaks of God's tender mercy toward weak and sinful people. Nothing reveals His beauty as does His tenderness to fallen people. It is like carved ivory (the King James Version calls it bright ivory). Polished ivory was rare and expensive. His compassion and His patience toward weakness are described as very rare and unusual, which indeed they are.

Isaiah 55:9 says, "For as the heavens are higher than the earth, so are My ways higher than your ways, and My thoughts than your thoughts." Typically, we quote that passage to mean God's wisdom, but this verse is not talking about wisdom when it says that God's ways are higher than man's as the heaven is above the earth. Instead, it refers to His ability to forgive weak people. There is no one on the earth who forgives weak people as God does. His ways are as high as the heavens are above the earth. This mercy is not God saying, "Well, boys will be boys. Go ahead and have a little bit more leeway." It is skillful mercy that brings us to repentance, purity and wisdom. It is not mercy that has no object in it, but it is strategic and as purposeful as mounting a sapphire stone. His creativity in showing His mercy brings righteousness and trains us in wisdom.

His Legs

IN ADDITION, *His legs are pillars of marble.* This attribute is the administration of His will and kingdom. The apostles are the pillars of His kingdom. They are the strength that holds up His church. Pillars in our churches are the individuals who provide strength through their endurance, wisdom, gifts and maturity.

His Countenance

HIS COUNTENANCE IS like Lebanon, excellent as the cedars. The countenance speaks of the impartation of God to His people.

> LORD, lift up the light of Your countenance upon us.
> —PSALM 4:6

When God shines His countenance on your heart He is imparting Himself to you. I picture the light of God shining down and touching your heart. When the light of God shone upon Mary, the Holy Spirit overshadowed her, and a very significant impartation occurred.

The Father wants to impart His affection for Jesus and wants us to love Jesus as He does. He has the ability to take weak flesh and infuse it with the divine character trait called godliness.

You can put your hand on somebody all day long and pray, but if the Holy Spirit does not move, you cannot impart anything. God, however, has an infinite power to impart His own character traits of wisdom, purity and passion into you. That's a unique ability that only God possesses that allows Him to place a deposit into the center of the human being.

HIS MOUTH

THE NEXT DESCRIPTION of Christ is this: *His mouth is most sweet.* This speaks of the communication of His intimacy. Jesus wants to impart spiritual intimacy. Spiritually, the Lord wants to release the kisses of His Word as the bride cried out for in Song of Solomon 1:2. This speaks of Jesus releasing the grace of intimacy by enlarging our capacity to receive more of God.

> How blessed is the one whom Thou dost choose, and
> bring near to Thee,
> To dwell in Thy courts.
> We will be satisfied with the goodness of Thy house,
> Thy holy temple.
> —PSALM 65:4, NAS

How blessed is the one God chooses to draw near to Himself. Seasons come when Jesus tenderly draws us near, but there are other times of prayer when we do not feel Him drawing us closer.

In certain respects, He is always near us, and we always have access to the throne of grace. Experientially, I know what it means to have prayer time when the nearness of God is on me. I also know what it means not to have the nearness of God.

The most powerful experience a human being can have is when God allows the human spirit to see even a glimpse of the heavenly Bridegroom. When God the Spirit releases His revelation to the human spirit, nothing is more pleasurable and more powerfully penetrating. It is more powerful than physical, mental and emotional pleasures. When the Spirit of God kisses our expectant hearts, we cry out like David in Psalm 19:10, saying, "More to be desired are they than gold, yea, than much fine gold; sweeter also than honey and the honeycomb."

God wants to communicate His sweetness to us, but He will only do so to those people who are reaching toward Him.

He also seeks us when we are unconverted in order to save us. He chases, ambushes and traps us until we say yes to Him. Once we are saved, the Lord still continues to draw us, because He wants us to seek Him. Those that make the Lord their magnificent obsession will be blessed with treasures and sweet things.

Proverbs 2:4–5 challenges the body of Christ to seek the Lord as silver. We must gain the knowledge of Him, for there are hidden things that God will only give to the hungry.

His mouth is most sweet. It is well worth the time and effort, the drawing back a little bit from the hustle and bustle and the revamping of our schedules to run after Him, because being kissed by the presence of God is sweeter than anything else in the human experience.

What a wonderful Bridegroom! Because of His blood that He shed for us, we will be getting to know Him for all of eternity, learning more about Him and experiencing the wondrous bounty of being His bride. This love for Him will consume the very nature of who we are. He is calling us today to a love for Him that is so consuming that we will lead others in the way. This flame of spiritual pleasure will either enrage, or it will ignite a greater love that burns within the people who are already touched by His love.

Draw me away! We will run after you.

—Song of Solomon 1:4

6

LONGINGS
OF THE BRIDE

Before that morning in my office when the Lord called me to proclaim the Song of Solomon and the message of the bride of Christ, I had always felt a deep longing to be consumed with more desire for God. I prayed often, studied the Scriptures and surrounded myself with great teachers and preachers by reading many books. But on that day as I knelt to pray in my office, little did I expect to receive a new direction that would result in experiencing an entirely new dimension of spiritual desire.

I began to pray because an unusual, quiet yearning had filled my heart. It grew as my heart was stirred, and it became an intense longing, a thirst that felt impossible to quench. "Lord, seal me. Put the fiery love in me. Seal me, Jesus. Put the love in me." As words of desire began to pour from my lips, the desire for God felt stronger and stronger, until it almost hurt. I began weeping, not from pain but from desire. But the longing for Christ only became more intense.

It was as if what I was experiencing was a divine vacuum that was actually drawing upon God Himself. That drawing brought His presence, His very heart, into greater and greater manifestation. As I touched the nearness of God, the desire intensified even more. Before long the room was filled with His wonderful, divine presence, and my heart was spilling over. I could do little more than continue to weep, at first from passionate desire, and later for joy and gratitude for His nearness, but for much more. I felt deeply grateful for who He is, His love, His mercy, His truth and perfection, and I felt more grateful still to know with greater certainty than I'd ever imaged that He loved me so much.

The desire for Christ the Bridegroom is a consuming, passionate fire.

Longings are a powerful force that receives from the spiritual and brings to the natural. Every believer already experiences powerful longings placed within him or her by God's creative design for a wonderful spiritual purpose.

In the last chapter we explored the attributes and characteristics of the Bridegroom God as seen from the viewpoint of a mature bride who is sustained by her love during a time of testing. Responding to our Bridegroom as the mature bride of Christ will satisfy the seven different longings that are in all of our hearts. In His sovereignty, God has placed these seven desires in us, and it is His will for these desires to be fulfilled by Him.

I call these seven desires the foundations of the bridal paradigm of the kingdom. These longings are also seven unique privileges that we have as the bride of Christ. These seven desires reflect seven different emotions in God's personality and are aspects of our own creative design, and these emotions are in us also. They illustrate what I mean by the superior pleasures of the gospel and what it means to be romanced by the Holy Spirit. Finally, these seven desires reveal our primary success in life, for regardless of our circumstances we will walk successfully when these longings are being stirred and met by the Holy Spirit.

The seven longings of the bridal paradigm are unique to humans; angels do not have them. Nowhere does Scripture suggest that angels have the capacity for affection. They experience joy and other emotions, but these are not the same as spiritual affections. Only humans have the capacity for the burning spiritual desire of affectionate love. God's capacity for burning affection is one of the most unique aspects of His character. Such spiritual affections cause our lives to reach great heights in the Spirit.

The capacity for affections exalts us in the glory of God when fulfilled in Christ, but this very capacity also can be our ruin. Deep affections and passions can be dangerous if not fulfilled in the right way. In other words, if we resist the Holy Spirit in our quest to fulfill our affections, they can also be very dangerous because they can bring us to the depths of perversion. An individual's capacity for burning desire, if refused, releases a terrifying capacity for destruction.

KNOWING WE ARE ENJOYED

THE FIRST LONGING of the human heart is to have the assurance that we are enjoyed by God while still spiritually immature. To be enjoyed by God is a necessary part of living right. God enjoys us even when we are in the midst of our immaturity and weakness. You cannot repent of or get free from this longing of the human spirit because God Himself placed it within you.

The idea of being enjoyed by God is difficult for some to

receive. Some say, "Maybe God will enjoy me in heaven, but never while I am on earth." Others admit that God may enjoy them on earth, but only if they are as spiritually mature as the apostle Paul.

But the truth is that God will enjoy us while we mature. The knowledge of this is a vital key to turning sincere desire into spiritual maturity.

We must not confuse God's enjoyment of us while we are maturing with His approval of every desire of our lives. Jesus enjoys me, while at the same time He disapproves of a single area of struggle in my life. It is not an all-or-nothing relationship. Some think that God either approves of all we do or disapproves of us entirely. This is simply not correct.

God loves and enjoys me while correcting me in various areas of my life. We must not confuse His correction with rejection. When He does correct me, it is because He loves me. If I feel enjoyed by God while I grow spiritually, still I know He will discipline various areas of my life. He does this in the overflow of His passion for me.

We must repent when we seek to fulfill this longing in an incorrect way, but we can never repent for having the longing. This longing will never go away, but it is satisfied by the revelation of God's extravagant passion for us and the revelation of the Father and the Bridegroom.

This longing to be enjoyed by God is also the seedbed for all the false religions of the world, for the devil exploits this human longing and brings many evil and false religions into existence.

Our spiritual health and maturity depend upon knowing that God enjoys us, for it addresses the fear of rejection within our hearts. The fear of rejection and the trauma of shame are the most powerful emotions in the human spirit.

Something powerful is awakened in our hearts when we truly know that God enjoys us, and we respond with abandonment in our commitment to God. Even a little knowledge of how much God enjoys us goes a very long way. When we feel enjoyed by the Father and cherished by Jesus the Bridegroom, something powerful is awakened in our hearts.

Without this understanding we become vulnerable to Satan as he lures us into traps, offering to meet this longing in false ways. In the bridal paradigm of the kingdom of God, this longing is first. The bride's love rests on the assurance that she is enjoyed and delighted in and that God pursues and wants her. We are most defined by the One who wants us.

The reason that we are successful is because the God of all the earth wants to marry us. He wants us as His eternal companion. My ministry may never be big. I may never have a lot of money, and I may never have a lot of friends, but the fact that Jesus desires and pursues me answers the greatest need in my heart to be successful. You are already successful in the most primary sense even if nothing else good happens in your life. He longs for you. The One whom the seraphim bow before wants you. Beloved, you are truly successful.

BEING WHOLEHEARTED AND PASSIONATE

THE SECOND LONGING that I associate with the bridal paradigm is a desire to be wholehearted and passionate. Our hearts were created as the seat of great desire and passion; therefore, experiencing this desire is also very important for spiritual health. It is not enough to know that God wants us. We also need to know that we are giving ourselves to Him with all of our hearts. Our God, who loves and gives with His whole heart, designed us with the need to be wholehearted. If we have nothing to die for, we'll have nothing to live for. We love to love Him. We enjoy loving Jesus with all our hearts. To be a hopeless hypocrite who is not a genuine lover of God is something contrary from being the person we were created to be. Living in a state of spiritual passivity and boredom makes us vulnerable to Satan's attacks. One of the greatest problems with the church in America is the lack of wholeheartedness.

Counseling ministries attempt to bring people to emotional wholeness, but if believers aren't called to wholeheartedness, they will never enjoy emotional health. Loving and serving with a whole heart pleases the Lord, but there is more to it than that. Many believers attempt to live in the grace of God without abandonment to God. They look for a way to understand grace that reinforces their carnal lifestyles. We need to experience grace that leads us to the joy of wholehearted living and loving. A wholehearted God designed me to need and to long to be wholehearted!

FASCINATED AND FILLED WITH WONDER

THE THIRD BRIDAL longing is the desire to be fascinated, to be filled with wonder, to be awestruck and to marvel. The secular entertainment world has exploited this longing in the human spirit, and it tempts us to answer this longing in all the wrong ways. I am not against all secular entertainment. That is not my point. But most of secular entertainment is a false attempt to answer a legitimate longing. Our fascinating God created us with a need to be fascinated. When we are not fascinated with Him, we become bored, spiritually dull and spiritually passive. Immorality, the love of money and bitterness toward people who hinder us from getting our desires filled can then move into our hearts and corrupt them even further.

Isaiah 4:2 says:

> In that day the Branch of the LORD shall be beautiful and glorious.

This verse concerns the church at the end of the age. The Word promises that the Branch of the Lord, which is a term for the Messiah in His humanity, will be seen in His beauty throughout the entire earth. The beauty of Jesus holds a powerful place in the End-Time strategy of God. The Father will use the beauty of Jesus at the end of the age to fascinate the End-Time church with Jesus. It will not be a bored church that exits the earth in power. The Lord will unlock the divine treasure chest, and the Holy Spirit will take the things that belong to Jesus Christ and give them to the church. We will experience divine entertainment at its richest with the human spirit awestruck by the beauty of God.

This was the number one theme of King David's life. In Psalm 27:4 he sought one thing all the days of his life—to gaze upon the beauty of the Lord.

> One thing I have desired of the LORD, that will I seek: that I may dwell in the house of the LORD all the days of my life, to behold the beauty of the LORD, and to inquire in His temple.

I have reflected upon this verse for many years, and I can see that the beauty of the Lord is a mountain that is far bigger than we might imagine.

> But God has revealed them to us through His Spirit. For

the Spirit searches all things, yes, the deep things of God.
—1 CORINTHIANS 2:10

The Holy Spirit searches the deep things of the beauty of God, and the Father has granted Him permission to impart aspects of this revelation to you and me. A billion years from now in heaven we will still be discovering new dimensions of the vast ocean of God's beauty.

Nonetheless, to ascend this mountain of discovery will require time in the Word of God, not just to study it, but to approach this revelation with a heart of devotion.

At times we need to approach the Scriptures academically because we must understand their context to better grasp what the writer meant. I believe in the academic approach to the Word. I lead a full-time Bible school in our church, but I tell our students that study is not enough. Our knowledge of the Word must be applied with devotion toward the Lord. In our study, our hearts must be in quest of new discoveries of the beauty and the knowledge of God. To live before God with even a beginning measure of awe completely changes the way we look at sin.

The beauty of the Lord reaches its pinnacle in the revelation of our Bridegroom King, our Messiah. The Bridegroom King is so beautiful that with this divine weapon the Holy Spirit will ravish the heart of the End-Time church.

I know in my heart that the Holy Spirit is going to raise up thousands to focus on preaching on the beauty of God, and in so doing He will cure the boredom of His people. Is the Lord calling you to be one of these preachers?

LONGING TO POSSESS BEAUTY

THE FOURTH LONGING that I identify as expressing the bridal

114

paradigm is the desire to possess beauty. We as members of the bride of Christ long to receive the impartation of the Bridegroom's beauty in our own lives. The beauty that God possesses is imparted to His people through redemption. We are adorned in the beauty of the Lord because He makes the redeemed beautiful. He will give us beauty for ashes. When we feel beautiful before God because of the glory of His presence instead of feeling ugly, marred by sin and hypocritical, something powerful is released deep within our hearts. Our beauty in redemption reaches its highest place of revelation in the unveiling of the bride of Christ.

There are several different dimensions of the beauty that God imparts to the church. There is physical beauty and spiritual beauty (along with it being temporal beauty in this age), and then there is eternal beauty in the age to come. Did you know that you will possess physical beauty forever beyond any of the angels of God? When Jesus became a man and God raised Him from the dead, the Father designed a body for Him. The capabilities of Jesus' resurrected body are unimaginable in beauty, far beyond the angels. A fragrance flows out of His body in heaven, and when He walks, that fragrance fills the city of God.

Do you know that Jesus is a human in heaven? He is fully God, but He is also fully human! It is staggering to me that He has a human mind in heaven. The mystery of Christ's two natures is far greater than my understanding. Nevertheless, Christ's two natures grant Him the capacity for knowledge and affection as a human.

Jesus Christ's resurrected body is the most beautiful body imaginable! Philippians 3:21 declares that the same resurrected body will be given to the saints.

Who will transform our lowly body that it may be

conformed to His glorious body, according to the working by which He is able even to subdue all things to Himself.

We will possess a beauty that is not merely spiritual. No only will we love God and walk in marvelous revelation, but we will also appear beautiful to others. The lights, colors, fragrances, supernatural abilities and tastes will be amazing. Along with possessing this beauty, we will be able to hear sounds, probably at distances.

This beauty touches us physically to some degree in our countenances when our hearts are renewed. A happy heart and a bright countenance physically transform us, and this kind of physical beauty is enhanced in heaven. Our physical beauty will be fully revealed in the age to come, but our spiritual beauty can increase much in this age. The ability to love, think and feel as God does begins now. The Lord will adorn His church with His own beauty in the days ahead.

Many passages in the Bible describe for us the beauty of the Lord. For example, Revelation 21:2 says:

Then I, John, saw the holy city, New Jerusalem, coming down out of heaven from God, prepared as a bride adorned [made beautiful] for her husband.

The Father has made beautiful a bride for His Son. The city of God is called the bride because of its inhabitants who govern it. When we stand before Jesus on the last day, we will feel and look physically and spiritually beautiful, because that is the way God intended for it to be.

It is the innate need to express through one's person the beauty of God that Satan attempts to counterfeit through natural efforts at vain beauty. I am not against pursuing natural beauty by working out in the gym, wearing makeup and the like, but I do give this one warning: These pursuits do not fully satisfy the heart's cry to be beautiful. It's proper to enhance one's physical beauty. Of course, there are boundaries, and when people attempt to answer their deepest longings to be beautiful through empty, carnal methods alone, they can end up with many destructive addictions in their hearts. Eating disorders, sexual addictions and many other destructive behaviors are related to a perverted attempt to fulfill this persistent and deep human longing to feel beautiful and to be beautiful.

But when our longing to be beautiful is fulfilled in God, because we are truly beautiful in God, then our hearts enlarge in power. Although only a measure of spiritual beauty is released in this age, a little goes a long way. It is powerful to feel spiritually beautiful before God—at least a little bit. I am well aware of my sins, struggles and weaknesses, but I also understand who I am as the bride. So I come before the Lord knowing that He enjoys me and fascinates me with His beauty. I feel genuinely beautiful before Him. This romance of the gospel frees us from the enslavement of inferior pleasures, and the domination of sinful pleasure begins to be broken.

The Longing for Success

THE FIFTH BRIDAL longing is the desire to be great, noble and successful. This deep human longing is answered by God as He enthrones us as His bridal partner throughout eternity. As the bride of Christ we have the highest position of honor and authority in eternity, a position far above all the angels. Jesus treats us as a bride with the dignity of a partner in God. Every check that God signs He expects us to cosign.

117

Romans 8:17 shows that we are His coheirs with divine authority.

> And if children, then heirs—heirs of God and joint heirs with Christ, if indeed we suffer with Him, that we may also be glorified together.

Jesus desires to share aspects of His rulership with His bride. Do you have any idea who you are? The final word of promise that Jesus gave to the seven churches of Asia was related to the bridal partnership wherein we will sit with Him in power, privilege and position as His eternal coheir.

Revelation 3:20–21 says:

> Behold, I stand at the door and knock. If anyone hears My voice and opens the door, I will come in to him and dine with him, and he with Me. To him who overcomes I will grant to sit with Me on My throne, as I also overcame and sat down with My Father on His throne.

When Jesus visited John on the island of Patmos, He returned in His resurrected body to show the apostle John the great promise of honor and power that is His ultimate desire for the church. As humans, we are the secret in God's heart. We are one class of His created order that will sit in God's presence throughout eternity.

The highest position of honor for all of God's creation is reserved for the bride who will partake of the wedding table of Revelation 3:20. The bride who sits at the table feasting with Christ is the one who sits with Him in the position of government and authority as well. These are two aspects of the bride's calling. In the Bible, only one table exists. Of course, there is the communion table of Psalm 23:5 where

God will "prepare a table before me in the presence of my enemies." But Revelation 19 tells more about what the table is; it's the wedding supper of the Lamb.

You are a member of eternity's aristocracy: the ruling class. Think of the ruling class of this nation. It's comprised of a small number of families, and many a young woman dreams of entering into wealth and power through marriage. But you are the aristocracy of the heavenly city because you married into the wealth and power of almighty God. Pursuing greatness to exalt ourselves out of God's will is sinful, but God has nevertheless ordained for you to be great in Him. Jesus never told His followers to repent of wanting to be great, for greatness is part of God's divine design for human beings. God created us to be great, and we will be forever with Him. Greatness in God is not defined by earthly circumstances—having money, friends, a ministry or good health. Greatness in God focuses upon His greatness and not on our own.

The thief on the cross must have been shocked when he stepped into paradise that very day. He had died a criminal without any money, friends and honor, cast off by society, but he stepped across that mysterious line in physical death and found out that in paradise he was honored like a king. Even the lowest believer is much higher than the angels. I can imagine him looking around and saying, "No one ever told me I was a king! I would not have stolen money if I had known that I was a king!"

The bride of Christ is the queen of heaven because she is married to the King of kings. Believers are priest and kings. As priests we are wholehearted lovers, but as kings we are indeed in the government of the city of God.

MAKING AN IMPACT ON OTHERS

THE DESIRE TO impact others is the sixth human longing that we will briefly look at. As the bride of Christ, we desire to impact others, to feel significant and to exhilarate others with good news of the gospel—the sixth longing. For example, when one of the blind men was healed at Jesus' meeting, imagine his joy in telling his blind friends about the meeting the following day. How exhilarating to bring that news to them! Imagine the joy as he informs his friends that another healing meeting is scheduled for the following evening.

The ability to make an impact on others is something that was given to us by God. When we do not have an impact on anybody, our spiritual lives lose their joy and freshness.

INTIMACY WITHOUT SHAME

THE SEVENTH BRIDAL longing is for intimacy without shame. The Bible says:

> Therefore a man shall leave his father and mother and *be joined* to his wife, and they shall become one flesh. And they were both naked, the man and his wife, and were not ashamed.
> —GENESIS 2:24–25, EMPHASIS ADDED

Adam and Eve were together, naked and unashamed. Adam and Eve were married partners in the flesh. But Christ and His church are married partners in the realm of the Spirit. The New Testament interprets this passage from Genesis as follows:

> "For this reason a man shall leave his father and mother and *be joined* to his wife, and the two shall become

one flesh."This is a great mystery, but I speak concerning Christ and the church.

—EPHESIANS 5:30–32, EMPHASIS ADDED

In other words, this verse refers to the marriage union between Jesus Christ and the church. Jesus Christ is joined to us, His adoring bride, in the most powerful expression of divine intimacy possible. To be naked and unashamed means that all secrets have been unveiled and there is no shame. God trusts us with the secrets of His heart, secrets He will not even give to the angels.

In 1 Peter 1:12, the angels look to the church to understand some of God's secrets.

> To them it was revealed that, not to themselves, but to us they were ministering the things which now have been reported to you through those who have preached the gospel to you by the Holy Spirit sent from heaven— things which angels desire to look into.

God does not entrust the angels with this information. Beloved, do you realize who you are? God has chosen you, His bride, to teach His secrets to angels.

AN INVITATION TO HOLY ROMANCE

THE HOLY SPIRIT invites you to enter into a romance, the magnificent love song of a heavenly Bridegroom and His waiting bride. This romance of the gospel will thrill your heart and satisfy the longings deep within you. This, my friend, is the key to happy holiness!

THEY SHALL BE ABUNDANTLY SATISFIED WITH THE FAT-
NESS OF THY HOUSE; AND THOU SHALT MAKE THEM
DRINK OF THE RIVER OF THY PLEASURES.

—PSALM 36:8, KJV

7

The Pleasure
of Holiness

Picture walking up to a homeless little boy and handing him a ticket for a wonderful vacation by the sea. He would stay at a five-star resort hotel, eat the finest foods that money can buy, sleep on a warm, clean bed and spend his days swimming in the crashing waves and building sandcastles on the beach.

The dirty little youngster takes the ticket from you and places it among other collected items in a corner of the large box where he sleeps at night to shelter himself from the rain and cold wind. Instead of eating hamburgers and fries, apple pie and ice cream, he curls up on a door stoop and eats spoiled meat he has gathered from the trash. He plays in the dirt, making mud pies and eating them as his dessert.

C. S. Lewis put it this way: "We are half-hearted creatures fooling about with alcohol and sex and ambition when infinite joy is offered to us. We are like an ignorant child who wants to go on making mud pies in a slum because we cannot imagine what is meant by an offer of a holiday at the sea."[1]

That's the choice we make every time we are confronted with a decision to say yes or to say no to this world. It looks tasty, it looks as if it will satisfy and it has in the past, but in fact it is spoiled meat. It's molded bread. It's mud pies for dessert.

The pleasures of God are a banquet set before us, a table of spiritual delights that once tasted deliver us from the emptiness of seeking earthly pleasures. The way to free the heart from the domination of sin is by delighting in God. Holiness is a superior pleasure that transcends anything that sin can offer us.

Holiness is not the result of gritting our teeth as we set our hearts to resist sin. If we try to fight sin primarily with prohibitions and threats, we will fail. The decision to say no to sin is itself energized by the experience of fascination in God added with the assurance of delight in eternity.

When we examine church history, we see that the theme of holiness has often been presented in a negative way. Churches throughout history have created endless lists of threats and warnings of the consequences of sin. Certainly, the Word of God teaches clearly about the consequences of deliberate, sinful rebellion. The Bible is full of don'ts and prohibitions, but these laws and rules were never designed by God to supernaturally transform the human heart and its affections.

A traditional approach of many preachers uses shame and fear to motivate people into keeping a list of dos and don'ts. But in the end, the allure of the immediate pleasure of sin is often more powerful than the fear of long-term consequences. Yes, church leaders must continue to forcefully present to people the consequences of sin, but we must do so realizing that this alone is not sufficient. Something more needs to be in operation.

Warning people about the social and spiritual consequences of sin will not cause them to reject pornography, greed, lying and cheating. In fact, when we are tempted to sin we usually already know the negative risks of shame that we face. Hearing harsher and longer sermons against the sins we lust after usually will not make much long-term difference.

Sin and Satisfaction in God

HAVE YOU EVER thought about why we sin? Sin produces immediate pleasure. It gives a physical, spiritual and emotional rush. We do not sin out of obligation. We sin because we believe that it will provide a pleasure that is superior to the pleasure of obedience to God. The power of temptation rests on a deceptive promise that sin will bring more satisfaction than living for God. The Word of God calls this promise the deceitfulness of sin or the deceitful lusts.

> Put off, concerning your former conduct, the old man which grows corrupt according to the deceitful lusts.
> —EPHESIANS 4:22

And again:

> Lest any of you be hardened through the deceitfulness of sin.
> —HEBREWS 3:13

We will only win the battle of temptation as we enjoy God. The secret to conquering sin is satisfaction in God. The Holy Spirit is setting forth the beauty of God in Jesus Christ so that we might become enticed by a holy affection whose power rivals the power of our sin.

125

SEEKING HEAVENLY PLEASURES

GOD MADE US spiritually, physically and emotionally needy people. In the depths of our hearts we long for happiness. We desire it, and we yearn deeply for pleasure. We are designed by God to be pleasure seekers. This in itself is not sinful; finding our pleasure in unrighteousness is what is sinful. The Bible says:

> In Your presence is fullness of joy; at Your right hand are pleasures forevermore.
>
> —PSALM 16:11

Prohibitions and threats do not result in holiness. This negative approach to holiness produces fruit that is neither lasting nor fulfilling. But we will stay committed to holiness that flows from the beauty and pleasure of living lives unto God. Experiencing the superior pleasures of living our lives unto God will cause us to seek more of the pleasure that's found in Him and less of the pleasures of the world.

This does not mean that we disregard the negative restraints in the Word of God. These glorious parameters are guidelines for living with passion for Jesus. They actually help to keep us in the presence of God where there is fullness of joy.

While it is important for us not to despise the prohibitions mandated in the Word of God, the fact remains that many threats or warnings given by preachers today are shame-based. Many preachers tell people, "If you do such and such, you will be exposed. You will be caught and humiliated in front of everyone. You will bring embarrassment to your family." Despite such warnings, fear of shameful consequences is still not enough to energize us to resist the pleasures of sin.

126

Our superior experience of God must be the primary motivation to resist sin. The fear of negative consequences cannot do this. Why? Because the temptation to experience the immediate pleasure of sin is usually more powerful than the fear of punishment. This fear of sin's consequences will not overpower the tendency in our hearts to sin. Instead, it will cause us to sin in secret, more creative ways.

WHY DO WE SIN?

WHY DO WE sin? We sin because we enjoy the pleasure it brings. John Piper says, "Sin is what we do when our hearts are not satisfied with God."[2] This statement helps us understand why the struggle for holiness must actually be the pursuit to stay satisfied with God.

God Himself designed us as very needy creatures. He placed within us great hunger and thirst—some of it emotional, some mental, some spiritual and some physical. All of these cravings within the human heart cry out to be satisfied. But God's presence is the only place where the hungry soul finds true satisfaction. In His presence is fullness—joy fulfilled and eternal pleasures overflowing.

In his book *Pleasures Evermore: The Life-Changing Power of Enjoying God,* Sam Storms says, "We must swallow up the flicker of sin's pleasure in the forest fire of holy satisfaction. The only thing that will ultimately break the power of sin is passion for Jesus. The only thing that will guard me from being entrapped by sin is being entranced by Jesus."[3] God is not glorified by recruits who want to help Him out. Our God is so completely full, so self-sufficient and so overflowing in power, life and joy that He glorifies Himself by serving us. The knowledge of God that transforms the heart is the knowledge by which we are ravished by the beauty of who God is.

HOLINESS AND PLEASURE

GOD DOES NOT call us to holiness to keep us from a life of pleasure. Holiness is not drudgery. Instead, God calls us to a holiness that fully releases infinite and perfect pleasure to us forever. The psalmist said, "At Your right hand are pleasures forevermore" (Ps. 16:11). These pleasures are imparted by God's right hand: His Son, Jesus Christ.

We do not glorify God when we arrogantly presume that we can give God what He doesn't have. He is most honored when we come to Him with an attitude that recognizes that all He does for us is intended to increase our satisfaction in Him.

The Word of God tells us about the choices Moses made.

> By faith Moses, when he became of age, refused to be called the son of Pharaoh's daughter, choosing rather to suffer affliction with the people of God than to enjoy the passing pleasures of sin, esteeming the reproach of Christ greater riches than the treasures in Egypt; for he looked to the reward.
>
> —HEBREWS 11:24–26

Moses had experienced the pleasures of the flesh that accompanied the riches and power of his position in Egypt, but he chose greater riches. He experienced something more pleasurable and beautiful than Egypt, something supernaturally attractive and altogether satisfying. As you press into the pleasures of holiness, like Moses, you will discover that none can fill the soul like Jesus.

BUT THE DAYS WILL COME WHEN THE BRIDEGROOM WILL
BE TAKEN AWAY FROM THEM, AND THEN THEY WILL FAST.

—MATTHEW 9:15

8

THE
BRIDEGROOM FAST

SINCE THE DAY in my office when God called me to proclaim
the glorious message of His bride to His people, my life
has changed dramatically. I've changed as well. I desired the
Lord with increasing fervency, but often I felt I was just not
breaking through into the greater reality of His Spirit for
which my heart longed.

At first I experienced times when I felt as if my prayers
were bouncing off the walls. I have often joked that I have
had more unanointed prayer per capita than anyone I know.

As I sought God to draw me into a greater depth of His
presence, I began to sense that God was speaking to me
about fasting. Because I have been personally called into
some different ways of living before the Lord, I was confronted by good people who were very upset by this. I began
fasting with a new intensity. When I first began to walk in a
new dimension of grace-empowered fasting, I didn't really
understand all that was going on, so I placed myself under a

gag order. I purposed to walk in this for at least two full years before I spoke of it publicly. I didn't preach on fasting for the first two years that I was walking in it.

When I starting spending increasing amounts of time in prayer, some of my friends expressed concern. I simply told them that what was happening to me in the area of fasting was not about them. It was not something that I was putting on them. I was obeying a divine invitation, and my weak, little, skinny heart began growing in Him a little bit.

So for two years, I said little about fasting. However, I have since felt released to call people forth to this very significant area of grace. In those two years of fasting, the Lord taught me about what I refer to as the Bridegroom fast. I discovered that fasting is a powerful spiritual tool that can turbo-charge our journey into the depths of God's presence. Fasting in grace will cause the little spark of hunger in our spirits to ignite into a roaring flame. Let me share with you some of the wealth of spiritual treasure that the Lord graced me with as He taught me to live a fasted lifestyle.

THE FASTED LIFESTYLE

AS YOU FEAST on the beauty realm of God and you become impatient for more of His presence, just salt the feast with fasting. Fasting is a divine catalyst that increases your capacity to receive more from the Spirit.

There are two primary types of fasts in the Bible, but many subcategories stem from them.

Although many believers understand fasting to be an Old Testament practice, fasting is still used often in the New Testament church. But Old Testament fasting was primarily used to avert disaster, either national or personal. For example, if a hostile nation was about to attack Israel, the Jews would sometimes call a fast to seek the Lord for His help against their enemies. In times of a personal calamity, an individual would fast, and the Lord would deliver him or her from the affliction. This paradigm of fasting is very biblical and even continues throughout New Testament times. However, this particular type of fasting is not the highest form.

THE BRIDEGROOM FAST

I SPEAK OF the Bridegroom fast. It is mentioned in Matthew 9:15 when the disciples of John the Baptist complained that Jesus' disciples did not fast. Jesus responded by saying:

> Can the friends of the bridegroom mourn as long as the bridegroom is with them? But the days will come when the bridegroom will be taken away from them, and then they will fast.

Have you ever felt that you just could not stand to go on living without more of Jesus Christ in your life? I have. It's for such seasons of spiritual hunger that God has given us the Bridegroom fast. It is a fast that enlarges our capacity to receive freely from the Spirit of God. Instead of having an external purpose such as averting a crisis, this kind of fasting changes us on the inside.

When you cannot live without something in God, some place of depth of communion in His love, then it is God's will for you to cry out for it with a new resolve and intensity. If you absolutely cannot live without a new depth in your intimacy with God, the Lord will usually increase your portion of it over the following months and years.

We receive spiritual tenderness and new discoveries of

intimacy with God more quickly and more deeply when we fast.

Jesus asked John's disciples the following question: "Can the friends of the bridegroom mourn?" Understand that fasting is not merely mourning for God, but also mourning for the Bridegroom God. At this point in His ministry Jesus knew that His disciples' hearts had become accustomed to His physical presence as He gazed into their eyes and communicated His affection, beauty and stunning wisdom to them every day. He knew that once He had died and ascended, fasting would help them recover some of the wonderful reality that they had experienced with Him in His physical presence with them.

Jesus knows the human heart and how it works. When Jesus was to leave, the Holy Spirit would minister to them in His place. The disciples would receive more of Jesus than they had already experienced through the power and presence of the Holy Spirit.

Christ knew that once He was gone, the disciples' desire, longing and lovesickness for Him would cause them to mourn to be close to Him as in the days that He walked with them. That hunger to recover that same sense of closeness to Him would prove to be a key to their intimacy, power, anointing and the fellowship of the Holy Spirit. The disciples mourned for more of Him after His death and resurrection. This new mourning for Him would motivate and empower their fasting. I call this fasting by the power of lovesickness.

Only Jesus could have thought of the unique paradigm to respond to spiritual lovesickness. Jesus combined the two seemingly divergent ideas into one. No other religion in the world has ever linked fasting to lovesickness.

SPIRITUAL MOURNING

WHILE JESUS WAS still walking the earth, the disciples felt the Lord's love for them, they experienced His embrace and they sensed His deep desire for them. Their hearts were captured by Jesus and completely dedicated to Him. They had burned all their bridges in the abandonment of devotion, and they could never go back to business as usual. They were the Lord's for life.

When the Bridegroom ascended into heaven, the ache of desire and the remembrance of intimacy stung their hearts with pangs of love's desire.

When He left them through His death and resurrection, they mourned the loss. That's what Jesus meant when He said that they would mourn and fast when He left the world. He was not talking about mourning over the nation. Jesus was referring to their longing for the same nearness with the Messiah Bridegroom. We could replace the word *mourn* with the word *lovesick*.

Jesus knew the disciples' hearts would desire more of Him. They would long for the opportunity to look into the eyes of Jesus and to feel the warmth of His nearness as in former times when they walked the hills of Galilee. However, God had a new plan to satisfy their longing. By the Holy Spirit, the Lord would release the fulfillment of their hearts' desire. As they would seek His comfort, they would again experience the previous satisfaction they had when He was so near to them. This would come about through the Holy Spirit revealing Christ through the Word. At that point, they would add fasting to the longing in their hearts, and their spirits would become tender in love.

This is fasting in the grace of God. This type of fasting will

135

be restored worldwide and will be vital to the forerunner ministry, which we shall look at in greater depth in the next chapter. Fasting is absolutely essential for developing a deeper experience of devotion for Christ. The Bridegroom fast tenderizes our spirits, helping us to receive freely and deeply.

If you are beginning to be stirred with lovesickness, remember that it takes God to love God. Only God the Holy Spirit can impart God's love in us for God. Even before we begin to regularly enter into this fast, the Word of God awakens in us a desire for deeper divine love.

This fast flows out of a desire that has already been awakened in our hearts for God. It results in an increase of that very desire. Even our desire to fast comes directly from Him.

You might read this and become intrigued by the beauty of God, even though you may have never previously considered the idea. This new way of thinking about God's affection might stir new emotions inside of you. This awakening of desire is the beginning of what leads us into this Bridegroom fast. Then the fast itself awakens even more desire, and this new level of desire leads us into even more fasting and more desire. It's like the saying, "The rich get richer."

PURSUING GOD WITH HOLY VENGEANCE

> Take heed what you hear. With the same measure you use, it will be measured to you; and to you who hear, more will be given. For whoever has, to him more will be given; but whoever does not have, even what he has will be taken away from him.
>
> —MARK 4:24–25

In this passage of Scripture we can see that we need to be careful about what vision in God we settle for. This is what

Jesus means by the warning to be careful what we listen to or what we buy into or settle for as our life's vision. As we are drawn to a greater revelation of God's beauty, we become lovesick for Him. As we cry out to God, expressing that we cannot live without more of Him, the treasures that the Holy Spirit imparts to us will take root and grow in our hearts as we value and pursue them with holy vengeance.

> And from the days of John the Baptist until now the kingdom of heaven suffers violence, and the violent take it by force.
>
> —MATTHEW 11:12

This does not speak of physical violence. In the context of this scripture, Jesus is using the word *violence* to sum up John the Baptist's radical love and obedience aided by a grace-empowered, fasted lifestyle.

Fasting is not just about food, but rather it is about a number of areas of our lives. Our fasting is never an attempt to try and get God to do something. Instead, we fast because God has already moved our hearts. This type of fasting is unfamiliar to some of us.

If you are fasting to create an image of how dedicated you are, forget it. Fasting should never be done as a show or to gain a reputation of being more anointed; fasting is an intensely private thing. Fasting is easily misunderstood, and there are many dangers when dealing with the subject of fasting.

Legalism is just one of these of dangers. Fasting to get God to pay attention to us is just one example of legalism because the motive is rooted in a misunderstanding of God's grace. We should fast because we know that God enjoys us and because we want our hearts to receive more of Him. That is grace-empowered fasting.

At this point in time, most people in the body of Christ are not ready for fasting. The holy violence that Jesus speaks of in Matthew 11:12 is a pursuit of God that is often disruptive in the way that we spend time and money, for example. Spiritual intensity disrupts our lives, our status quo, our circle of Christian friends and the pace of spiritual growth at which we are moving.

As you press into fasting, those around you may take a step back and say that you are weird. The fasted lifestyle is appropriately called violent.

ISSUES OF JUDGMENT

WHEN TWO PEOPLE move at different rates of growth and maturity in God, they often begin to judge one another. When you begin to move into the fasted lifestyle, expect disruptions in some of your domestic relationships and even in your kingdom relationships.

If everyone grew in Christ at the same pace, and if everyone always used wise and humble language, we could avoid many conflicts and misunderstandings. However, we all know that this is simply not the case. Christians are going to continue to mature at different rates, and we often communicate what is happening in our hearts in imperfect ways that we later regret.

WISDOM WILL BE VINDICATED BY HER CHILDREN

JESUS SAID:

The Son of Man came eating and drinking, and they say, "Look, a glutton and a winebibber, a friend of tax

138

collectors and sinners!" But wisdom is justified by her children.

—MATTHEW 11:19

Essentially, Jesus was saying that the wisdom of John's fasted lifestyle would be openly displayed by the fruit of his life in the days to come, especially when he stood before God in eternity. In other words, Jesus was saying that even though they criticized John as demonized, the wisdom of his life would be apparent to all one day. Some might doubt and even snicker when John was finally thrown into prison, but before it was all over, the wisdom of John the Baptist's life would be openly displayed for all to see. Its fruit would be displayed before all. Jesus might have even continued the thought by saying that his works were so great that they would not be fully manifested until the age to come.

FRIENDS OF THE BRIDEGROOM

Then the disciples of John came to Him, saying, "Why do we and the Pharisees fast often, but Your disciples do not fast?"

—MATTHEW 9:14

John the Baptist taught his disciples to fast. I don't believe they were being proud or contentious by asking Jesus this question. I think they were sincerely confused and wanted to understand why Jesus apparently allowed this compromise in the life of His disciples.

And Jesus said to them, "Can the friends of the bridegroom mourn as long as the bridegroom is with them?

> But the days will come when the bridegroom will be
> taken away from them, and then they will fast."
>
> —MATTHEW 9:15

In Matthew 9:15, Jesus asks them if the Bridegroom's friends should mourn as long as the Bridegroom was with them. Here, to John's disciples, Jesus called Himself the Bridegroom for the very first time in the Bible. However, Jesus did not publicly indicate that He was the Bridegroom until His last sermon (Matt. 22). Jesus is aware that John the Baptist was looking for the Bridegroom, so He gave John's disciples a little hint by calling Himself the Bridegroom.

By calling Himself the Bridegroom twice in this passage, Jesus was directly relating Himself to the One of whom John had spoken earlier.

John the Baptist said:

> He who has the bride is the bridegroom; but the friend
> of the bridegroom, who stands and hears him, rejoices
> greatly because of the bridegroom's voice. Therefore this
> joy of mine is fulfilled.
>
> —JOHN 3:29

In this passage of Scripture, John the Baptist calls himself a friend of the Bridegroom. When Jesus refers to Himself twice as the Bridegroom, the apostles of John must have realized that John had been speaking of Christ.

That spiritual reality of being a friend of the Bridegroom did not just belong solely to John, but it was a spiritual reality that belonged to them as well. Although John's claim to being a friend of the Bridegroom was personal and singular, Jesus' declaration about friends of the Bridegroom was plural, and it included John's disciples.

Jesus said that as long as the Bridegroom was present there was no need for mourning or fasting. The reason that they would fast in the future would be because of longing for the Bridegroom God. They would not just mourn for God. They would mourn for the Bridegroom God because they had become accustomed to Him in the person of Jesus Christ. The hearts of the people of God would now be expanded in the revelation of the Bridegroom.

Jesus Christ knew that when He left them they would not just yearn for revival to come forth. They would yearn for Jesus Himself. They would desire the personal embrace of the Bridegroom God.

THE DANCE OF THE LORD

VOLUNTARILY ENTERING INTO the loving embrace of the violent One is the dance of the Lord. The violent Lover is the One who violently laid aside the form of God and gave up all of His rights to bear the pain and suffering of others. This is the kind of spiritual violence that Jesus speaks of Matthew 11:12 when He says that the violent take the kingdom by force.

Fasting for power is in the Bible, but that is not what this scripture refers to. It is not just an invitation into greater realms of power. It is far more than that. The Bridegroom fast is an invitation into greater realms of intimacy with the Bridegroom through the work of the Holy Spirit.

The Bridegroom fast will be used by the Holy Spirit to unlock deep places of our hearts in spiritual intimacy. Fasting enables us to see spiritual things that we normally could not see. The increase will not happen overnight. In fact, it may not even happen much in the first months, but our level of intimacy with the Lord will grow over years and seasons. We will see more this year than we did last year, and more next year than we did this year.

Fasting increases the tenderizing of our hearts by removing the spirit of dullness and deadness off of us so that we feel the presence of God and His love in a more discernable way. I stress the word *feel* because, although feelings are not our primary concern, they do make life far richer and make even difficult circumstances easier to handle. Undoubtedly, you will not feel God's presence every minute of every day, but when you embrace the fasted lifestyle, you will feel Him more than you do now. I can assure you of that.

Your spiritual commitment and intensity will also grow as a result of fasting. Fasting in fellowship with the Holy Spirit helps protect us from discontentment, coveting and fleshly cravings. Fasting will lead to a change of your emotional chemistry. You will, for the most part, no longer desire to have the things that you once wanted. This is because fasting intensifies your detachment from worldly concerns. The strange thing about fasting is that it requires doing nothing instead of doing something, for when you fast you don't eat, don't work, don't talk and so on.

This is the ultimate state of the foolish and weak things of this world, confounding the so-called wise things of the world. (See 1 Corinthians 1:27.) Fasting does not require ability, education or money. In fact, anybody can fast before God because all you do is nothing.

Areas in which we are compromising will begin to decrease because fasting releases grace that insulates us from discontentment, complaining and griping that is so prevalent throughout the world. Fasting literally begins to unlock and release those negative feelings that have been ruling our hearts and ruling us. This powerful spiritual tool strengthens our spiritual identity in God and weakens our fleshly identity. The presence of God released through fasting also helps to break the bondages of self-absorption so common in today's world.

In addition to learning to fast, I encourage you to put your cold heart in front of the holy bonfire: the Word of God. As you begin to read the Bible, express your love to God continually, which will help create an atmosphere of spiritual intimacy. Determine to press into spiritual intimacy for many years to come, and do not reevaluate the effects until you at least reach the one-year mark. I do not believe that there will be one person at the one-year mark who will not realize radical inward changes.

We really cannot expect to press into a greater depth of the Spirit if we go up to God's bank casually and say, "I want the deep things of Your wealth, but I only have a few minutes to spend with You." The Lord and Creator of the earth might respond as follows: "If you want the deep things of My Spirit, then I will freely give them to you based upon the hunger of your heart." Spiritual hunger always has a certain force of intensity to it. When we cannot live without depth in God, then God will give it to us in due season.

EXPLORING THE FASTED LIFESTYLE

IN DEVELOPING A fasted lifestyle, you may want to be aware of some other types of fasting and their benefits to those seeking a deeper walk with God. Fasting is a powerful tool to use when seeking God's direction for your life.

In times of crisis

This type of fasting was done in times of crisis, especially in the nation of Israel. This kind of fast may be in response to a military or national crisis. Many times, when an army was about to wipe them out, the Israelites would all fast for a day or two. Crisis fasting is very biblical, and the Old Testament doctrine carries over into the New Testament. This type of fast would be appropriate when there is a crisis in your church, family or personal life.

Protest fasting

The second type of fasting is a fast of protest. People who are not necessarily Christians also fast to voice their opposition to a national evil. Often called a hunger fast, protesters fast to stir an entire nation. For example, in Ireland some years ago, twenty guys went on a sixty-day water fast, and a number of them died. Though God does not want us to do anything that touches the spirit of lawlessness, fasting is one very intense way for godly people to protest.

The protest fast sometimes results in a breakthrough in power. When your church, or even your own life, is barren, this type of fasting can bring a breakthrough.

Jesus spoke of this in Matthew 17:21 when He said, "However, this kind does not go out except by prayer and fasting." When the barren powerlessness of the hour is not acceptable to you any longer, enter into a protest fast. Fasting is a way to protest the barren state of our lives or of the church. We also can protest our lack of power to bring deliverance to others.

We often associate fasts of protest with healing and revival. In this age of lawlessness, do not protest with your mouth by talking and complaining. Instead, go into a fast of protest, and watch how God answers.

Fasting for direction

This type of fasting is seen in Acts 14:23:

144

So when they had appointed elders in every church, and prayed with fasting, they commended them to the Lord in whom they had believed.

Before they laid hands on the elders, they sought the direction and the blessing of God.

A Word of Caution

Certain dangers are involved with fasting. Ill-advised fasting can lead to eating disorders and a host of other physical and spiritual problems. To produce good fruit, fasting must be done with a biblical foundation and in the grace of God.

Followers of the occult also fast seeking satanic power. False religions, such as Hinduism, for example, ordain long fasts for purification as well.

I encourage you to enter into fasting with caution and to be sure that you are fasting for the right reasons. Jesus Christ also warned His followers not to fast for the wrong reasons.

Moreover, when you fast, do not be like the hypocrites, with a sad countenance. For they disfigure their faces that they may appear to men to be fasting. Assuredly, I say to you, they have their reward.

—Matthew 6:16

When I talk to people about fasting, I tell them to be careful not to boast to their friends that they are fasting. You may even consider fasting in secret, according to Matthew 6:6.

But you, when you pray, go into your room, and when you have shut your door, pray to your Father who is in the secret place; and your Father who sees in secret will reward you openly.

A totally different emotional chemistry is released when nobody knows that you are fasting. With nobody there to pat you on the back, you won't have to struggle over sorting out your motives. Fasting in secret actually unlocks your heart far more quickly than when other people know what you are doing.

Jesus commanded us to fast in secret. Secrecy helps us to keep our motives pure.

SERVING THE LORD
WITH PRAYER AND FASTING

IN LUKE 2:37, we see that Anna served the Lord with fasting and prayer in the temple.

> And this woman was a widow of about eighty-four years, who did not depart from the temple, but served God with fastings and prayers night and day.

My prayer, and I know it is going to happen, is that God would revive the serving of the Lord with prayer and fasting in the temple. I'm not suggesting that you should fly over to Israel and live there for the next thirty years. I am talking about fasting in the context of serving God's purposes on earth.

A look at Simeon and Anna also shows how God significantly uses older people in serving the Lord through continual prayer and fasting. In our day, God is going to use people who are retired. If you are nearing retirement, your strength has been given to you for this hour, and God has freed you from many things. There's not a more powerful force in the earth than that of senior saints who have time and passion for Jesus.

> And behold, there was a man in Jerusalem whose name was Simeon, and this man was just and devout, waiting for the Consolation of Israel, and the Holy Spirit was upon him. And it had been revealed to him by the Holy Spirit that he would not see death before he had seen the Lord's Christ. So he came by the Spirit into the temple. And when the parents brought in the Child Jesus, to do for Him according to the custom of the law, he took Him up in his arms and blessed God.
> —LUKE 2:25–28

Simeon and Anna are wonderful testimonies of the significant things that can happen when senior saints in the body of Christ enter into the ministry of prayer and fasting. I believe that this type of ministry will occur again among young people, but there will always be a strong, dynamic contingent of elders who are praying and fasting across the world.

The young people will be bonded to them as to mothers and fathers in the Spirit. Adolescents will look into the eyes of their elders in the Lord and will wonder why they feel such a strong spiritual connection between them. Young people will look up to you, senior citizen, and say, "I don't know why, but I really like you." You may smile knowingly because you were the one who birthed these young people into the kingdom of God.

No matter what your age, your most successful years are still ahead of you.

BRIDEGROOM FAST BECOMES JOYFUL FEASTS

Thus says the LORD of hosts: "The fast of the fourth month, the fast of the fifth, the fast of the seventh, and the fast of the tenth, shall be joy and gladness and cheerful feasts for the house of Judah. Therefore love truth and peace." Thus says the LORD of hosts: "Peoples shall yet come, inhabitants of many cities; the inhabitants of one city shall go to another, saying, 'Let us continue to go and pray before the LORD, and seek the LORD of hosts. I myself will go also.'"

—ZECHARIAH 8:19–21

This passage of Scripture also refers to the Bridegroom fast. He says your fast will be turned into joyful, spiritual feasting before the table of the Lord. When you feast in God's presence, you are feasting at His table. I believe this points to the joyful feast we will share together at the marriage supper of the Lamb. Indeed, He turns our mourning into great, inexpressible joy.

I am totally convinced that God will raise up a ministry that wholly serves the Lord with prayer and fasting because it is on fire with holy passion for a Bridegroom God. This passion and longing for Him will be expressed and strengthened through the fasted lifestyle.

THE VOICE OF HIM THAT CRIETH IN THE WILDERNESS. PREPARE YE THE WAY OF THE LORD, MAKE STRAIGHT IN THE DESERT A HIGHWAY FOR OUR GOD.

—ISAIAH 40:3, KJV

9

THE
FORERUNNER
MINISTRY

JOHN THE BAPTIST came out of the wilderness one day
wearing camel hair, eating locusts and honey and crying
out the generation before the first coming of Jesus Christ:
"Prepare ye the way of the Lord."

Today an entirely new generation is rising up out of the
wilderness of obscurity to proclaim the same message: Make
the way straight for Christ's Second Coming.

This powerful cry from the wilderness to the people of
God is the End-Time ministry of the forerunner.

THE LAST GENERATION

YOU ARE TRULY unique by virtue of the time in which you are
living. You may actually be living in the final prophetic
moments preceding the coming of the Lord. Can you fathom
what this means for you? Can you begin to imagine how this
reality might shape your identity and destiny? The power of

this reality grows in me a little more each year. When this reality gets hold of you, it will literally change the way you live your life.

The last generation before Christ returns will witness the greatest demonstration of God's power in history. There are three "supernatural generations" that enjoyed an unusual call of destiny in God's prophetic timetable described in the Scriptures. I define a "supernatural generation" as a generation in which the majority of God's people witness the power of God on a regular basis. This term cannot be found in Scripture. The idea is biblical, but the term is my own.

Throughout all of the redemptive history of mankind, the power of God has been revealed intermittently, a little here and a little there. For example, during the time of David, the power of God would come upon him, and his army would win a great battle. Afterward, the men would go back home to business as usual. For this reason, I would not consider David's generation to be one of the supernatural generations.

Let's look at three generations in Scripture that fit the criteria of supernatural generations: the generation of Moses, the generation of the apostles and the generation of the Second Coming.

THE GENERATION OF MOSES

I CONSIDER THE generation of Moses to be a supernatural generation. During the time of Moses, amazing miracles occurred, miracles that were so powerful they changed the natural order of things and brought Egypt, the mightiest nation on earth, to its knees. Most Christians are very familiar with the account in the Book of Exodus of the powerful judgments that demonstrated unimaginable supernatural might.

In the first of the ten plagues of Egypt the water was turned to blood. Streams, rivers, ponds and pools became undrinkable. Similar ensuing disruptions of the natural order affected everything—lice multiplied, insects swarmed, frogs overran the land and many of the Egyptian people died. Even the sun and the sky were affected.

These kinds of supernatural events are experienced corporately by entire nation of Egypt. Such miracles were designed to break the power of the world dominance of Egypt. Usually such miracles release God's judgments against unrighteous nations, and those judgments concurrently release God's chosen people to worship Him. This was God's purpose to liberate Israel from Egypt.

THE GENERATION OF THE APOSTLES

THE GENERATION OF the apostles is another supernatural generation. The generation of the apostles was very different from the generation of Moses. During the time of the apostles, miracles touched individual lives and manifested God's compassion in restoring in the grace of God. In both the generation of Moses and the generation of the apostles I use Moses and Paul respectively to describe their entire generations, but the miraculous is imparted to far more people than just these two individual men. The power of God was released in the midst of the redeemed in both Moses' and Paul's generations.

Although Christ calmed the storm and multiplied the loaves and fishes, the overriding purpose of the power of God that was manifested through the apostles was to restore individual lives.

THE GENERATION
OF THE SECOND COMING

THE THIRD GENERATION in our study is the generation of the Second Coming of the Lord. During this generation the kinds of powerful displays of the miraculous released through Moses and those witnessed through the apostles will be combined and multiplied on a global dimension. The combination of miracles that affect the natural order in the earth and miracles that restore individual lives will affect the entire world. These two kinds of miracles will be unleashed on a global level, thereby bringing in the great harvest just before the Lord returns.

I personally believe we are in the early days of this final generation. If this be true, then you and I are fortunate enough to be a part of this blessed generation. It may appear like business as usual right now, but I believe we are at the beginning of the supernatural generation that will experience the greatest demonstration of power ever witnessed in history. It looked like business as usual during Moses' fortieth year in the wilderness tending sheep. I'll bet Moses never dreamed that he was about to operate in the power of God in a way that would cripple an empire.

It probably felt like business as usual the week before the Lord called Peter, James and John from their nets. They probably never dreamed they would soon be moving in the supernatural power of God as they became fishers of men. At times the Word of the Lord comes suddenly, changing a person's entire destiny within moments of time.

When God's power flowed through Moses, the former shepherd, Pharaoh became helpless as a child. His army could do nothing to stop the power of God at work through Moses.

In the end, Pharaoh's army was destroyed in the Red Sea.

Those who oppose God at the end of the age will face this same kind of awesome power, but the signs and wonders will be multiplied globally.

> As in the days when you came out of the land of Egypt, I will show them wonders; the nations shall see and be ashamed of all their might; they shall put their hand over their mouth; their ears shall be deaf. They shall lick the dust like a serpent; they shall crawl from their holes like snakes of the earth. They shall be afraid of the LORD our God, and shall fear because of You.
>
> —MICAH 7:15-17

As with Pharaoh, wicked leaders at the end of the age will be brought down to the ground. They will be humiliated and stricken, and they will be absolutely stunned by the power of God.

Wicked leaders will become afraid of the Lord our God. Micah says, "They shall fear because of You!"

Because of God's mercy, only those who resist the Lord need to be afraid. This passage of Scripture in the Book of Micah goes on to speak of the One who delights in mercy.

> Who is a God like You, pardoning iniquity and passing over the transgression of the remnant of His heritage? He does not retain His anger forever, because He delights in mercy. He will again have compassion on us, and will subdue our iniquities. You will cast all our sins into the depths of the sea.
>
> —MICAH 7:18-19

These prophetic men and women who will loose the

power of God on nations need not be afraid. They can be confident of the fact that "He delights in mercy."

> And it shall come to pass in the last days, God says, That I will pour out of My Spirit on all flesh; your sons and daughters shall prophesy, your young men shall see visions, your old men shall dream dreams.
>
> —ACTS 2:17

We know that the last days began on the Day of Pentecost. But only the down payment of God's power was released back then. Ongoing visitations of God's power have been released over the last two thousand years since then. But before the Lord's return, a deluge of God's power will be poured out on all flesh, upon the redeemed in every nation of the earth. God's people, some more than others, will begin to experience the realm of the supernatural. They will prophesy, see visions and dream dreams. The realm of the invisible will open up as a deluge of the Spirit is poured upon all. When this happens in fullness, every single believer in the earth will begin to experience the realm of the supernatural anointing.

> I will show wonders in heaven above and signs in the earth beneath: blood and fire and vapor of smoke.
>
> —ACTS 2:19

Wonders in the heavens above, signs on the earth beneath and blood, fire and smoke—these are what Moses experienced. The last generation will be used to release the same mighty signs and wonders. We will see blood, fire and smoke. The sun and the moon will be impacted. Just as in the time of Moses and the apostles, these miracles will impact an entire generation.

Two Witnesses

THE SCRIPTURES GIVE us an idea of what this kind of power is going to look like.

> If anyone tries to harm them, fire comes from their mouths and devours their enemies. This is how anyone who wants to harm them must die. These men have power to shut up the sky so that it will not rain during the time they are prophesying; and they have power to turn the waters into blood and to strike the earth with every kind of plague as often as they want.
> —REVELATION 11:5–6, NIV

Understanding these two strange figures in the Book of Revelation is important. I believe they are forerunners, as John the Baptist was, preparing the way for the Second Coming of the Lord. We are not given the names of these two End-Time prophets—the ultimate forerunners.

The forerunner ministry will reach its zenith in these two prophets when the spirit of Elijah is released in its fullness in them, just as it says in the Book of Malachi. In this hour of time they will do the miracles of Moses.

> Behold, I will send you Elijah the prophet before the coming of the great and dreadful day of the LORD.
> —MALACHI 4:5

They have power to shut the heavens (Rev. 11:6). Now that sounds like what happened to Elijah when no rain fell after he prayed. These prophets will pray, and no rain will fall in the days of their prophesying. As with Moses, these two prophets will have power over the waters to strike them and turn them to blood. Their own wills will be lost in the will of God. Therefore, they will not strike in plagues apart from the mercy of God. It is a statement of the ultimate place of partnership with the Lord.

The angel Gabriel appeared to Zacharias and prophesied concerning John the Baptist, who was soon to be born. Gabriel declared that John would function in the spirit and power of Elijah. (See Luke 1:17.) This very spirit of Elijah will be manifest in fullness in the generation the Lord returns.

PARTNERING WITH GOD

PEOPLE WHO FUNCTION in this dimension of power will enter into partnership with the Lord even in the arena of God's temporal judgments. (See Psalm 149.) Being part of releasing the judgments at the end of the age may seem like a difficult concept to grasp, but remember that Moses did just that.

Yes, I believe there will be an army of worshiping intercessors that will loose vengeance on nations. These prophetic intercessors will operate in various measures of the anointing, yet in a lesser degree than the two witnesses. Nevertheless, the power of God manifested through them will be substantial because they will have a forerunner spirit upon their lives.

THE REVELATION OF THE BRANCH OF THE LORD

AS THE DYNAMIC events at the end of the age begin to unfold, it's important to remember that you will not be going through these things alone. Isaiah 4:2–6 is one of my favorite Old Testament prophecies about the end of the age. It speaks of the Branch of the Lord—the Messiah. This is an important passage for the forerunner ministry.

> In that day the Branch of the LORD will be beautiful and
> glorious, and the fruit of the land will be the pride and
> glory of the survivors in Israel.
>
> —ISAIAH 4:2, NIV

The entire chapter of Isaiah 4 is like a table of contents describing all the dimensions of the glory of God in the generation when the Lord appears. The revelation of Jesus as the Branch of the Lord in His beauty before all the earth is the spring from which all other revelation on this subject flows. The Branch of the Lord is used five times in the Old Testament to describe the second Person of the Trinity. This phrase illustrates how Jesus in His humanity grew and how His influence spread across the ancient Jewish world.

Because of who God is, He should never have to grow in influence. Nevertheless, He chose to humble Himself in His Son when He became a man. He was a branch that started as a twig and grew in understanding and wisdom. His influence spread out, and through partnership with His redeemed He bears fruit with all the other branches that are connected to Him. (See John 15.) Even though He was God, He submitted to accomplish His redemptive objective. The relationship between the Branch and the fruit speaks of partnership, a vital union of voluntary lovers.

In the last days, the Father will reveal His glory through the Branch of the Lord. In Psalm 27:4, David was electrified as he entered into the tabernacle where the glory of God rested over the ark.

> One thing I have desired of the Lord, that will I seek:
> That I may dwell in the house of the Lord all the days of
> my life, to behold the beauty of the Lord, and to inquire
> in His temple.

159

Although he was a mighty general and ruler, David unveils the bare essence of his soul's motivation. He was essentially saying, "I neither live primarily to be king nor to go battle. My primary goal and reward in life is to sit for long hours gazing at the beauty of the Lord."

David was swept away by the beauty of the Lord, and he wanted most to sit in the temple every day and to gaze upon Him. From there he would ask the Lord about everything that was on his heart.

The beauty of the Branch will once again be the center and the focus of the End-Time church. I believe that the End-Time church will realize the promise of the tabernacle of David, which was where he gazed upon the beauty of the Lord. I believe End-Time believers will see the beauty of the Lord behind the veil. One way we will experience God's glory will be through worship of a depth that we have never even imagined. We will worship the Lord, and the beauty of the Lord will be unveiled to the human spirit through the Word of God. Entering into His glorious presence will become a part of our lifestyle, similar to what David experienced in his life. I also believe that some us will have dreams and visions of the beauty of the Lord.

Jesus Christ will stun you with His beauty as He joins you to Himself as a vine and the Branch. In partnership with Him, you will bear His fruit that glorifies the Father.

> Then the LORD will create over all of Mount Zion and over those who assemble there a cloud of smoke by day and a glow of flaming fire by night; over all the glory will be a canopy.
>
> —ISAIAH 4:5, NIV

There will be a tabernacle for shade in the daytime from the heat, for a place of refuge and for a shelter from the storm and the rain. These are magnificent statements, beckoning us to come to Him in prayer and fasting.

The cloud and the smoke by day and the shining of a fire by night remind us of the anointing of the Holy Spirit that accompanied the leadership of Moses. Isaiah 4:5 does not refer to the eternal age to come, because God promises to send such a glorious presence to divinely shelter His people from a storm breaking forth over the earth. I believe that saints all across the cities of the world will gather together during these days to seek the Lord in unity. The cloud of glory and smoke of God will be in these citywide gatherings as these saints minister to the Lord continually.

Interestingly, smoke also appeared when Isaiah was commissioned as a prophet. (See Isaiah 6:4.) The smoke of God, which is the glory of God, filled the temple. I believe that like Isaiah, we too will see the smoke of glory witnessed by Isaiah. I believe that the fire of God will rest on us as well, as it did upon the Israelites in the days of Moses.

> "However, the days are coming," declares the LORD, "when men will no longer say, 'As surely as the LORD lives, who brought the Israelites up out of Egypt,' but they will say, 'As surely as the LORD lives, who brought the Israelites up out of the land of the north and out of all the countries where he had banished them.' For I will restore them to the land I gave their forefathers."
> —JEREMIAH 16:14–15, NIV

Similar occurrences to what happened in the Old Covenant will happen again in greater measure at the end of the age.

JUDGMENTS OF THE LAST DAYS

Multitudes, multitudes in the valley of decision!
For the day of the LORD is near in the valley of decision.
The sun and moon will grow dark,
And the stars will diminish their brightness.
The LORD also will roar from Zion,
And utter His voice from Jerusalem;
The heavens and earth will shake;
But the LORD will be a shelter for His people,
And the strength of the children of Israel.

—JOEL 3:14–16

This passage in Joel prophesies a day of judgment and decision for all of the earth's people. Revelation chapters 9 and 16 expand the vision even further, warning that the awful plagues and terrible judgments of that day will destroy a third of the earth's population.

God is about to shake Planet Earth. He has promised once more to shake not only the earth, but also the sky above. The writer to the Hebrews wrote:

> See that you do not refuse Him who speaks. For if they did not escape who refused Him who spoke on earth, much more shall we not escape if we turn away from Him who speaks from heaven, whose voice then shook the earth; but now He has promised, saying, "Yet once more I shake not only the earth, but also heaven." Now this, "Yet once more," indicates the removal of those things that are being shaken, as of things that are made, that the things which cannot be shaken may remain.
>
> Therefore, since we are receiving a kingdom which cannot be shaken, let us have grace, by which we may

serve God acceptably with reverence and godly fear. For our God is a consuming fire.

—HEBREWS 12:25-29

God's own people will be strategically placed. His power will be upon them, and through them He will release His mighty judgments as He did through Moses.

Jesus said:

To be sure, Elijah comes and will restore all things.

—MATTHEW 17:11, NIV

In this scripture Jesus tells us that Elijah is coming and that he will restore everything. The anointing, or the ministry gift, that was upon Elijah's life will be seen in the earth once more. This mighty prophetic anointing will lead to the restoration of all things as God promised. Is Elijah one of the two witnesses? I don't know, and I refuse to speculate on such important issues when the Lord has not specifically revealed them to me. But when the Elijahs do show up, it will be quite obvious who they are.

A down payment of the spirit of Elijah rested on John the Baptist. However, the fullness of this power will not be manifested until the two witnesses are functioning in ministry. I have prayed that God would raise up a million forerunners to prophesy End-Time events to the church.

I encourage you to study Exodus chapters 7 through 12 to gain a deeper understanding of End-Time events as seen in the miracles of Moses. The ten plagues, for example, help us understand what is still to come. Such plagues will occur again, according to the Book of Revelation, although the order in which they will come remains unclear to me. (See Revelation 8; 9; 16.)

Again, Jesus said:

> Most assuredly, I say to you, he who believes in Me, the
> works that I do he will do also; and greater works than
> these he will do, because I go to My Father.
>
> —JOHN 14:12

This End-Time generation is described more often in the
Word of God than any other generation.

God chose to describe this generation more than any
other because of its uniqueness in redemptive history and
because of its role in God's divine End-Time strategy. What an
amazing reality! Why would God pick one generation to
describe in His Word more than all others? God placed the
End-Time generation in a unique role and position in all of
human history.

Why is this generation so significant? It is the most popu-
lated generation in world history, for one reason. Consider
this: If one billion people get saved in the great harvest at the
end of the age, then there will be more of God's people on
earth than in heaven. You and I are truly the apple of God's
eye, and we live in a very unique time in history.

THE GREAT HARVEST

I PERSONALLY BELIEVE we will see a billion souls saved in the
great harvest. By statistical calculations, if one billion people
are saved, there will then be more of God's people on earth
than in heaven. I believe the release of God's judgments on
the earth and commissioning of forerunners to help get the
church ready by telling her what to expect will be integral
components of the great End-Time harvest.

You are part of the most unique generation in all of human

history. Your generation will witness the greatest demonstration of supernatural power ever seen. Your generation is the most described by God in His Word, and your generation is made up of more people than all other generations combined.

God is up to something—and we are at the end of the age. The glory of God and the storm of divine judgments are about to break forth over human kind, and your generation has a powerful role to play. For you were born for such a time as this.

For Zion's sake I will not hold My peace,
And for Jerusalem's sake I will not rest,
Until her righteousness goes forth as brightness,
And her salvation as a lamp that burns.

—Isaiah 62:1

10

THE
HEAVENLY SYMPHONY

I BELIEVE THAT THERE is no greater sound to the Lord than that of His church worshiping on earth together in unity with His orchestra above that fills the eternal city with heavenly music. Right now the Holy Spirit is drawing God's instruments together to form a beautiful symphony that flows in a divine score of worship, prayer, devotion and supernatural passion for God. He is calling the church to make a place for long and lingering worship and prayer. God will establish full-time intercessors, the modern-day Annas and Marys of Bethany, in local churches around the world. These individuals will be recognized and released to wait upon God full time.

In Kansas City, we have formed the International House of Prayer to answer this call. It all began for us in May 1983 when the Lord audibly spoke to us to establish a twenty-four-hour-a-day prayer ministry here in Kansas City. At that time, the Lord made it clear that we were to establish a night-and-day prayer ministry that reflects some of the principles seen in the tabernacle of David, the divinely inspired order of worship that King David established. We knew that we were to wait upon His timing before actually beginning to do this twenty-four hours a day.

Sixteen years later, at the beginning of 1999, God confirmed beyond doubt that we were to launch this prayer ministry in May 1999. At the time I was the pastor of Metro Christian Fellowship in Kansas City, and the Lord helped us by sending a fantastic new senior pastor, Floyd McClung, to allow me to fully dedicate myself to the new International House of Prayer. On May 7 of that year we dedicated a building about one mile from our church. It has a meeting room that seats about two hundred people. Around the clock, seven days per week, musicians play instruments, singers proclaim scriptures and prophetic songs, intercessors stand in spiritual watch and people join together in the presence of God to pray as the Spirit of the Lord moves them. We have lined the walls with tables so that people can read, write, work and meditate in the House of Prayer, which is a place prepared for His manifest glory to rest on us.

From around the world God has sent full-time intercessors to us who are fully committed to serve God as Anna did in the temple through prayer and fasting night and day. Many of them regularly dedicate forty to fifty hours each week to ministering to the Lord at the House of Prayer. All of them raise their own financial support as missionaries who serve the Great Commission through intercession. I am really blessed to see how the invitation of the Lord is going forth and people are responding with their hearts, commitments, time and finances. Our night watchmen are my heroes. They are the dedicated men and women who have committed themselves to the graveyard shift, and night after night, week after week, month after month, they minister to the Lord in the wee hours of the night. I am so thankful to be a part of this and to see the people responding with such eagerness and earnest dedication.

We conduct eighty-four two-hour prayer meetings a week, which equals one hundred sixty-eight hours, or twenty-four hours a day for seven days. Each prayer meeting is led by a worship team. The music has not stopped in over one year. We pray regularly that the fire of this prayer altar will never go out before Jesus' Second Coming.

We take this concept from the command given by God to Moses:

> And the fire on the altar shall be kept burning on it; it shall not be put out. And the priest shall burn wood on it every morning, and lay the burnt offering in order on it...A fire shall always be burning on the altar; it shall never go out.
> —LEVITICUS 6:12–13

So often the invitation of the Lord goes forth to a church or ministry, and then a year or two goes by and the people simply never respond to the Lord with a yes. They may analyze the invitation, talk about it and compare notes with one another, but they never move upon it. Instead of letting this invitation from the Lord fall to the ground, many people have said yes and wholeheartedly have dedicated themselves to this effort. Currently we have over one hundred full-time intercessory missionaries, and another one hundred are in the process of raising their own support to relocate here to help. Our vision is to form teams from these full-time intercessors and send them out to cities across the earth to start twenty-four-hour-a-day Houses of Prayer in the cities to which God leads them.

On May 7, 1999, we dedicated our new building and began taking steps to implement round-the-clock intercession. Our goal was to move to a twenty-four-hour schedule within twelve months, but we were actually able to do so within four months. On September 19, 1999, we had a full schedule of worship teams that enabled us to begin the twenty-four-hour-a-day schedule. Assembling of worship teams, singers and intercessors like this is truly powerful. God has given His people tremendous conviction to reorder their lives to do this full time. In the coming years, I am confident God will do this in many cities and towns around the globe.

We do not cancel the prayer meetings for vacations, holidays or birthdays. Our enemy, the devil, never takes time off, and neither do we. As I said earlier, each week is broken up into eighty-four prayer meetings where between fifteen and one hundred people are continually ministering to the Lord, no matter what the time of day or night. A key component of this ministry is the anointed prophetic music that fills the air during each and every meeting.

We believe that hundreds of churches will become involved in this in the future. We envision that one thousand to two thousand people will be gathered at each prayer meeting in the future.

Even in our first year of small beginnings, occasionally having only ten to fifteen people at some of the prayer meetings still has a spiritual impact upon the larger church. We must not despise the day of small beginnings. The very presence of a twenty-four-hour-a-day intercessory ministry in Kansas City is significant to God. People are moved and inspired by twenty-four-hour-a-day prayer, even in its weakness and immaturity. When I have shared this vision and testimony with other local pastors, some have been gripped by the idea. I told them how rough and tough the prayer meetings are sometimes. But many pastors and people who hear this vision still respond with supportive answers like, "But it's happening. It's happening, and we want a ministry like this in our city!"

When we share this vision with other churches, more of them want to become involved. In fact, interest is growing around the world as many different ministries are currently sharing this vision in print and at conferences.

The very fact that this ministry is going twenty-four hours a day has a catalytic impact upon other people who hear about it. First, it creates divine jealousy. I talked to one pastor in Asia who has a twelve-thousand-member church. In response to hearing about what we are undertaking, he said, "We have to do one. We have to do one. If you can do this by the grace of God, then so can we. If you are doing one, we have to do one! Will you bring a team to help us to get started now?"

At many conferences where I have shared this vision, I talk to pastors from all over the nations who respond by saying, "This is radical. We have to do one."

Other pastors are encouraged to make the attempt. They say, "If you can do one, surely we can do one, too." That is the impact we want. It is surprising and exciting to see the tremendous groundswell of inspiration and courage that God is releasing about the House of Prayer. Our own House of Prayer is not mature or strong yet, but the very fact that we are doing it has a catalytic impact.

I believe that it will be common to hear of twenty-four-hour-a-day prayer meetings springing up all over the earth. In fact, I believe that before the Lord returns, this will be happening in most of the cities of the earth.

I look for people who are also doing this. We share ideas about how the Lord is leading His people to pray, intercede and minister to Him. Oftentimes I implement certain things the Lord has shown others to do in their ministries, and vice versa. Piece by piece the Lord, by His Holy Spirit, is reestablishing the order of worship that was established by David.

I know that we are merely touching the bare beginnings of what the Holy Spirit will do. Night-and-day prayer ministry will be a global phenomenon orchestrated by the Holy Spirit. For this restoration to occur in a city the Lord will actively intervene in the midst of His people. This powerful reality brings joy to people who are not even involved in the House of Prayer. There's a comfort, joy and thankfulness that arises at the thought of a prayer furnace that burns twenty-four hours a day in your own city.

ALL DAY AND ALL NIGHT

THE SCRIPTURES CLEARLY show that God's promise to release the fullness of the Holy Spirit's blessings is only fulfilled in the context of night-and-day prayer. Many people become dismayed and say, "The promises are not taking place." They do not realize that God's conditions must first be in place, and night-and-day prayer is part of His conditions.

The fullness of God's promises will be released only after the condition of night-and-day prayer is met. Because of this, these twenty-four-hour prayer ministries are not only necessary, but they are also inevitable. We know this will happen because in His Word, the Lord Himself has told us that He is setting the watchmen on the wall. This is part of the Lord's heartbeat, and it will come to pass. Our Savior, the Chief Apostle who oversees the Great Commission, is the same eternal intercessor who sits at the right hand of the Father. Jesus the Intercessor will see to it that intercession burns night and day in the cities of the earth.

It is more than inevitable; it is glorious. There has been a distinct increase of the Holy Spirit's global prayer strategy during the last twenty years. To see this, we only need to look at the amount of literature on this subject that has been produced and sold in the Christian bookstores across the Western world. All around the world the Holy Spirit is stirring God's people and revealing His prayer strategy to this unique generation before He returns. Our goal is to see the divine order of worship restored. This order of worship exists in perfection in the heavenly symphony around God's throne, the place of perfect spiritual worship and truth.

King David established a worship order in his generation that reflected some key principles that exist around the throne. Our goal is not to seek to imitate King David's model of worship. No, we want to experience the heavenly reality. King David only touched the best of the Old Covenant earthly reality. Why do we care about David's worship insights? We can study what God showed David to get a better glimpse of the heavenly reality. I encourage people not to overemphasize David's model, but merely to use it as a launching pad to peer into heavenly worship.

This one dynamic is what the Lord has called us to birth at the International House of Prayer in Kansas City. Birthing other components of God's overall prayer strategy is being led by many other ministries. I know that our mandate from the Lord is just a sliver of the giant strategy that the Lord Himself is orchestrating in the last days. Our divine invitation to touch some of the Davidic principles of worship and prayer is glorious, yet we realize that it is only a small part of the whole picture in the hands of the Lord.

The worship and prayer that went forth in 1000 B.C. according to the Davidic model of prayer was led by singers and musicians who knew how to function in the prophetic spirit. The worship model that occurred in the tabernacle of David was a prayer ministry that emphasized being led by worship leaders, musicians and singers who are bold in the prophetic anointing.

HIS BURDEN IS EASY

I SPEAK OF intercessory worship because there is an interaction between worship and the speaking of the prayers. Something wonderful happens during the singing of prayers and the speaking of the prayers when the Spirit of God is upon the music. Prayer is easy. And because prayer is easy, people can pray much longer and more often than they could in the past. Prayer becomes refreshing and enjoyable!

Intercession without anointed music can sometimes be like working in a rock pile. I have done it for years. Just three people praying in a room for hours without the refreshing of anointed worship teams can sometimes truly feel like the hard labor of a rock pile—at least that has been my experience. That rock pile may bring a few moments of inspiration here and there, but this kind of prayer without music can also feel like a difficult and heavy calling. But when you add the anointed harp, God's music—now that's a different story!

> David, together with the commanders of the army, set apart some of the sons of Asaph, Heman and Jeduthun for the ministry of prophesying, accompanied by harps, lyres and cymbals. . . . All these men were under the supervision of their fathers for the music of the temple

174

of the LORD, with cymbals, lyres and harps, for the ministry at the house of God.

—1 CHRONICLES 25:1, 6, NIV

With God's music, as recorded in 1 Chronicles, the prophetic spirit comes upon musicians and singers, and the intercession becomes enjoyable.

I don't have faith for twenty-four-hour-a-day prayer in the cities all around the world if it's not mixed with anointed music, because it's just too hard to pray for long hours without the refreshing that comes with the music.

Then He spoke a parable to them, that men always ought to pray and not lose heart.

—LUKE 18:1

Jesus warned us not to faint in regard to prayer. This very thing has happened. Many believers in the Western world do not have a regular prayer life. Most churches in the Western world do not even have regular prayer meetings. In addition, midweek prayer services held in many churches are often sparsely attended. The result is that the church is fainting in prayer.

Let me tell you the good news. The fainting spirit is going to be replaced with anointed prayer that soars to the heavens and exhilarates intercessors in the process. I am convinced that the fainting spirit in the church will be replaced with the prophetic spirit model of 1 Chronicles, with elements of the Davidic model.

The Lord has honored us, together with other groups, to be pioneers in this. I would rather be at the International House of Prayer than anywhere else on the earth. That is how everybody should feel about where God has placed them.

To have a full impact, the prayer ministry must go hand in hand with other ministries, like missions, cell groups, outreaches to the poor, training centers and other aspects of church life. One without the other is not enough. The symphony of the Lord must come together. All of the one hundred full-time staff of International House of Prayer are required to be committed tithing members of local churches. The night-and-day prayer meeting is not enough. We long to see the local church exploding with evangelism that comes through anointed preaching with signs and wonders regularly taking place. The House of Prayer exists in part to change the spiritual atmosphere of a city. With twenty-four-hour-a-day prayer, the same sermon that resulted in ten new converts will result in one thousand as the spirit atmosphere is changed through night-and-day worship and prayer.

NIGHT AND DAY

I have set watchmen on your walls, O Jerusalem; they shall never hold their peace day or night. You who make mention of the LORD, do not keep silent.

—ISAIAH 62:6

"I have set watchmen." Here the Lord is speaking in the prophetic sense, and He is looking at the future as though it is accomplished and complete.

These watchmen, or you could call them intercessors or worshipers, are the people who cry out night and day. In the context of the Scriptures, watchmen can be prophets in other places, but these watchmen lift their voices and hearts night and day. The Lord is setting watchmen. It is a sovereign act when the Lord woos the hearts of weak, normal people like you and me and sets us on the wall.

176

SET UPON THE WALL

THIS WALL IS a figurative wall of protection for the church and a wall of blessing. You are being set upon the wall when your heart is moved by God. You know you have been set when you have been wooed, convinced and established by Him.

The Lord is serious about setting His watchmen in place. I look at the word *setting* in two different ways. I see two large categories of the setting of the watchmen. The first group is made up of people whose primary calling is not intercession, but something else. Their calling may be pastoral, evangelistic or administrative, or it may be in helps ministry.

I do not want to give the impression that one calling is higher than another. The greatest ministry is the one God has called you to. For example, if God has called you in His wisdom and kindness to the gift of helps, don't despise your calling by imitating the ministry of another. We all need to embrace our calling because it is the highest calling for us, one established by the wisdom of God who knows our frame so well.

Burnout comes when we try to operate in another person's calling. However, this setting of the watchmen may not be your primary function in the church, but you may be called to do it on occasion. There will be intercessors in the House of Prayer who will participate once a week because their primary call is to another kind of service.

Even one two-hour prayer meeting per week is no small thing. If you attend one prayer meeting each week that lasts two hours, in one year you will have prayed one hundred hours. Wow! That is no small feat—especially when your own efforts are multiplied across an entire city.

Thousands of people praying together one hundred hours

a year, now that is serious. However, there also will be another important group of watchmen who will form the foundation. This group of watchmen will be comprised of those called with a similar calling and anointing as Anna in the temple and Mary of Bethany. They are the ones whom the Lord will set upon the wall literally night and day, and prayer and worship will be their all-consuming function. Both groups are essential for the church to flourish.

ANNA AND MARY

> Now there was one, Anna, a prophetess, the daughter of
> Phanuel, of the tribe of Asher. She was of a great age, and
> had lived with a husband seven years from her virginity.
> —LUKE 2:36

Anna and Mary of Bethany were two full-time watchmen set upon the Jerusalem wall. They represented two different dimensions of the grace of prayer. The calling upon Anna and the calling of Mary of Bethany transcend gender and age. This calling is for males and females, young and old. These two dimensions describe an anointing, a calling and a focus upon a person's life.

In the generation in which the Lord returns, the Holy Spirit will bring the Annas and the Marys of Bethany forward and raise up a place for them in the End-Time purpose of God. The vast majority of Christians will not be called to this, but this group will make a significant difference in the End-Time church. I believe that it is possible that maybe less than 1 percent of all Christians will be called to this intensive type of ministry.

Anna speaks of the spiritual warfare, intercession and fasting. These are people whose main focus is to open the windows of blessing and tear down the spiritual walls of resistance. They are full-blast intercessors and spiritual warriors who are committed to fasting.

The Marys of Bethany will enjoy great grace for prayer and worship, but it will be very different. We can read about Mary of Bethany in Luke 10. She was an extravagant worshiper. Though she was not really an intercessor in the traditional sense, she did intercede. Along with that, Anna worshiped extravagantly, but the Marys of Bethany change the atmosphere of the cities and churches that they are a part of by being extravagant lovesick worshipers.

They can be male or female, young or old. We have a number of Marys of Bethany on our worship teams, both male and female. They change the atmosphere, releasing the beauty of the Lord. God has placed them in the midst of the people as a tender fragrance of the beauty of the Lord.

For centuries the Catholic church as well as the Eastern Orthodox church has always made room for the Annas and the Marys. Typically, monasteries for males and females, old and young, provided a place for night-and-day intercession and worship. The Catholics believed that the presence of such burning flames created a preserving grace for the church and society as well.

This current calling to be intercessory missionaries linked to God's plan throughout all of church history. Since this is such a radical idea for some Protestant believers, it's important to realize that the Holy Spirit has been doing this for many years. This is not something new to God. The apostle Paul urged young Timothy to provide financially for the widows who were willing to take vows of devotion to continual prayer.

> Now she who is really a widow, and left alone, trusts in
> God and continues in supplications and prayers night

and day.... And these things command, that they may be blameless.

—1 TIMOTHY 5:5-7

Even if the Annas and Marys never speak to anyone, their very presence creates a type of grace that preserves the church.

Unlike the Catholics, the Protestant church has not provided a place for these ministers. Many Protestants kind of scratch their heads and wonder, "What are we to do with such folks?" The Protestant denominations reacted to the ways in which they felt the Catholics missed the mark. For unfortunately many of these Catholic monasteries have lost the connection between night-and-day prayer and the Great Commission. They also lost touch with the surrounding societies in which they lived. But despite the disconnection, there was still a preservation, or a holding back of sin, because of their existence. Nevertheless, the impact of this level of devotion in prayer is much greater when a vital link with the Great Commission is maintained.

One of my favorite people in church history is a twelfth-century monk who lived in France. Bernard of Clairvaux is a brilliant example of a monastic leader who established night-and-day prayer that resulted in countless millions being born again through his preaching that was confirmed with great signs and wonders throughout Europe.

Throughout history, God has raised up many Protestant and Pentecostal women who have devoted their lives to prayer without a formal position in the church. Paul Cain's mother is one of the best examples I know. She labors long hours in prayer for revival and to see God's blessings released on Paul's prophetic ministry.

180

This glorious calling to devoted prayer has been a powerful tradition that began with the widows who served under Timothy and has bridged every denomination and movement in church history throughout the ages. I mention this since this calling may seem too radical to some believers who imagine that such a lifestyle is new and unproven in Scripture and history.

The Lord wants us to have Marys and Annas connected with apostolic teams that plant churches and win neighborhoods to Christ. It is important that these parts of the church work together.

Anna

ANNA—WHAT AN interesting woman! She served the Lord (ministered to the Lord) with fasting and prayer night and day. The word *ministered* is often exchanged with the word *serve.*

> And this woman was a widow of about eighty-four years, who did not depart from the temple, but served God with fastings and prayers night and day.
>
> —LUKE 2:37

What an unusual idea for a woman to minister to the Lord in prayer and fasting. Anna was probably about seventeen or eighteen years old when she was married, and after seven years she was widowed. So beginning in her early twenties she began ministering to the Lord night and day. At eighty-four years old, sixty years later, Anna was still faithful in this! She was constantly in prayer in the temple.

This is not just a call to older people who have retired from their secular jobs. Anna was a young woman in her earlier twenties when she began to do this.

What a woman! Beloved, in this very hour the Lord is wooing the Annas of the End-Time church, and He personally is setting them into their place. This calling is not reserved only for Catholic monks. The Protestant church must call the Annas forth, find a place for them, honor them and find ways of releasing them into their calling.

THE ANOINTING OF MARY OF BETHANY

> Now it happened as they went that He entered a certain village; and a certain woman named Martha welcomed Him into her house. And she had a sister called Mary, who also sat at Jesus' feet and heard His word. But Martha was distracted with much serving, and she approached Him and said, "Lord, do You not care that my sister has left me to serve alone? Therefore tell her to help me."
>
> And Jesus answered and said to her, "Martha, Martha, you are worried and troubled about many things. But one thing is needed, and Mary has chosen that good part, which will not be taken away from her."
>
> —LUKE 10:38–42

Mary of Bethany is pictured three times in the New Testament: Luke 10, John 11 and again in John 12. Interestingly, every time Mary is pictured in the Scriptures she is sitting at the feet of Jesus. The Holy Spirit placed her in the ministry of an extravagant lover waiting upon the Lord.

The Holy Spirit is presently commissioning the Annas and the Marys of this age. He is commissioning them, calling them and wooing them. He is identifying them within their own hearts.

MAKE A PLACE FOR THEM

GOD IS COMMISSIONING these intercessors at the same time He is calling believers to the twenty-four-hour prayer ministry. I believe that God is encouraging leaders, such as myself and others, to call forth Annas and Marys in the church today. Whether Catholic, Eastern Orthodox or Protestant, loving Jesus is the only requirement the Holy Spirit is looking for. God wants the church overall to stand up for those called to live like Anna and Mary. We must stop neglecting them.

To understand them, the body of Christ must first learn how to respect and support these individuals. Historically, Protestants have resisted such callings, considering them odd. We have feared that the Annas and Marys might get everyone to stop evangelizing in the Great Commission. Some churches want these people to move on because they do not know what to do with them.

We do not need to fear that people will spend too much time in the prayer room. If they get out of balance, know that filling their time with the Word and prayer will position them to hear God's corrective voice to them.

What about the fear that such people will develop lazy lives of religious isolationism? When was the last time you prayed eight hours a day? These intercessors are not lazy people. Work is accomplished in the prayer room, and it's certainly not a place to cop out from life. Though we enjoy God's presence, it is still hard work to focus on prayer for long hours in the work of intercession.

Some people feel threatened by these believers because they are afraid of feeling inferior if they get in place. The answer is not to get rid of them but to become secure in who you are in the Lord. Be secure in your own calling. Your calling is the highest calling for you. The vast majority of Christians will not be in that place of being an Anna or a Mary, but I believe that even in the Protestant Church we will at last learn to honor and release them. We are going to make a place for them. They are going to fit in somewhere.

The Lord may be calling you to be an Anna or a Mary. You may be saying to yourself right now, "That's really who I am!" If so, new strength will rise up within you to help you understand your spiritual identity. God will give you a bold new determination and ability to dismiss other options. I know a little about this because it happened in my own life, and I have a very clear sense of personal identity in this calling.

There is great power in having settled into the identity into which God has called you in the body of Christ. The Marys and Annas will not accomplish much all alone. But when they are linked relationally together with apostolic teams in local churches, the body of Christ working together in unison will form a glorious symphony releasing heavenly blessing and power.

Even them I will bring to My holy mountain,
And make them joyful in My house of prayer.
Their burnt offerings and their sacrifices
Will be accepted on My altar;
For My house shall be called a house of prayer
   for all nations.

—Isaiah 56:7

11

THE TABERNACLE
OF DAVID

M Y HEART MELTS when I think about the Song of
Solomon, and my heart soars when I think about the
tabernacle of David. The spiritual principles of the tabernacle
of David are treasures that I meditate on, pray about and dis-
cuss often with my friends and colleagues.

I get so excited just talking about the tabernacle of David. I
absolutely cannot wait to see how God unfolds the restoration
of this powerful revelation in our generation. I love the fact
that the Lord has called me to provide senior leadership to a
twenty-four-hour, citywide prayer ministry that seeks to
operate in the spirit of the tabernacle of David. What a blessing
this is! God certainly knows how to put a desire in our hearts
and then fulfill it way beyond our hopes and dreams.

As God has unfolded His plan for building the International
House of Prayer, He has also given us a greater depth of understanding about the tabernacle of David and how to implement
some of its components today. One of the primary passages,

187

but not the only one by any means, is in Acts 15:16–17:

> After this I will return and will rebuild the tabernacle of
> David, which has fallen down; I will rebuild its ruins, and
> I will set it up; so that the rest of mankind may seek the
> LORD, even all the Gentiles [nations] who are called by
> My name, says the LORD who does all these things.

This portion of Scripture was delivered to us by the apostle
James when he was settling the great Jerusalem council crisis
about the Gentiles. The debate was over whether or not the
Gentiles should be circumcised according to the custom of
Moses before they could be saved (vv. 2, 5).

Peter had been led by the Spirit to the home of Cornelius
the centurion. As Cornelius's friends and relatives listened,
the Lord gave him the answer to a debate. Peter opened his
mouth, and God broke in with power:

> "To Him all the prophets witness that, through His name,
> whoever believes in Him will receive remission of sins."
> While Peter was still speaking these words, the Holy
> Spirit fell upon all those who heard the word. And those
> of the circumcision who believed were astonished, as
> many as came with Peter, because the gift of the Holy
> Spirit had been poured out on the Gentiles also. For they
> heard them speak with tongues and magnify God.
>
> Then Peter answered, "Can anyone forbid water, that
> these should not be baptized who have received the
> Holy Spirit just as we have?" And he commanded them
> to be baptized in the name of the Lord. Then they asked
> him to stay a few days.
>
> —ACTS 10:43–48

This had already occurred when this big Jerusalem council was in progress in Acts 15. Interestingly, James answered the dilemma by quoting an unusual prophecy from Amos 9:11:

> On that day I will raise up the tabernacle of David, which has fallen down, and repair its damages; I will raise up its ruins, and rebuild it as in the days of old.

Although James used this scripture to prove that Gentiles are saved by grace, a number of other points are powerfully made in this powerful passage. Of all of the verses that could have been used, the Holy Spirit selected this obscure passage in Amos 9:11 to refer to the time when God would fully restore the tabernacle of David. The initial down payment of this prophecy began in the first century. However, the fullness of it does not occur until the End Times, the generation of the Lord's return.

Acts 15:16-17 describes the way in which God will bring all of the nations of the earth to the gospel. James made a very significant point for our generation right now. The tabernacle of David will be restored fully so that the Great Commission can be accomplished. The Bible refers to all of the nations on earth today.

> After these things I looked, and behold, a great multitude which no one could number, of all nations, tribes, peoples, and tongues, standing before the throne and before the Lamb, clothed with white robes, with palm branches in their hands, and crying out with a loud voice saying, "Salvation belongs to our God who sits on the throne, and to the Lamb!" All the angels stood around the throne and the elders and the four living

creatures, and fell on their faces before the throne and worshiped God.

—REVELATION 7:9–11

Of course, what is described here has not yet occurred, so we know that this will not be complete until the final generation of natural history.

UNDERSTANDING
THE TABERNACLE OF DAVID

JUST WHAT IS the tabernacle of David? It is the church of Jesus Christ in mature unity and in full victory reaping the great harvest under a citywide apostolic anointing and authority.

In the Old Testament, Melchizedek was a priest and the king. Although it was strictly forbidden to bring these offices together into one office under the Old Covenant, the office of Melchizedek was both a priestly and a kingly ministry. David, Moses and the Messiah are also examples of the combination of these two types of ministries. But when Uzziah attempted to walk in both offices, leprosy broke out in his body.

These offices, which under the Old Covenant were forbidden to be joined, are actually commanded to be joined together in the New Testament. The priestly and the kingly offices were joined together in the New Testament because Jesus walked in both. He came in the flesh as the full embodiment of combining the kingly and priestly offices. Nevertheless, in a foreshadowing of Christ's mighty ministry, David brought the two offices together in the tabernacle of David.

In its most abbreviated form, the priestly portion ministers to the Lord as a worshiper, crying, "I love You. I love You. I love You." The kingly portion, on the other hand, fulfills the mandates to subdue and defeat the enemies of God. The

Great Commission is a kingly task in the same way that worship and intercession are priestly functions. Priestly ministry is God-ward. Kingly ministry performs the mandate of the kingdom by defeating the enemies of God on the earth. Worship and intercession are priestly components. The kingly component is pictured in King David as he defeated the enemies of God around Israel.

In the New Testament, we do not use the terms *priestly* and *kingly* often. We see them used in the Books of Revelation and 1 and 2 Peter, but usually these words are replaced by the words *prophetic* and *apostolic*. I call the prophetic ministry an incense ministry of worship, prayer and hearing God. It combines the warring intercession with the "I love You" of worship. It is like the incense of our hearts ascending upward to God's presence with His prophetic word returning it back to us. The kingly ministry is the apostolic mandate to fulfill the Great Commission and to defeat the enemies of God.

In today's church our primary focus has been on kingly duties such as winning our neighborhoods to the Lord and bringing the nations into the harvest. This is fantastic and worth giving our best to. Nevertheless, we cannot overlook the priestly dimension as emphasized in the tabernacle of David. This is extremely important because I believe that God will restore the priestly function of the tabernacle of David before the fullness of kingly power comes into manifestation.

Our prayer ministry in Kansas City is just one of many ministries in this city. Citywide prayer ministries are merely catalysts to the release of the spirit of prayer upon the entire church. Therefore, it's important to remember that the entire church is God's House of Prayer, made up of all the local churches around the world that have an anointing of prayer.

Some individuals do not understand the larger spectrum of

the two combined ministries of the tabernacle of David, and therefore they consider that through prayer alone they are fulfilling the tabernacle of David. No, the tabernacle of David includes reaching the nations for Christ in power and evangelism as well as night-and-day prayer. We must not limit our understanding to the prayer side of David's tabernacle.

RESTORING THE TABERNACLE OF DAVID

WHEN DAVID TOOK the throne in Israel, the temple had not yet been built. The tabernacle of God, the tent that housed God's presence and represented His supernatural anointing and divine favor upon the nation, had fallen into disuse. Although the city of Jerusalem had already been established as Israel's holy center, the ark of the covenant was being stored in an individual's home after previous battles had nearly lost the ark to the people of Israel altogether.

The ark of the covenant actually represented the divine presence of God with His people. As the priests traveled through the wilderness with Moses, they carried the ark before the company of people upon poles according to carefully laid out instructions. When the Israelites made camp, the priests would set up the ark in the tabernacle, close the curtain between the ark and the people, and then the glorious presence of God would fill the temple as the priests ministered.

After David became king, he determined to bring the ark into Jerusalem.

> Then David consulted with the captains of thousands and hundreds, and with every leader. And David said to all the assembly of Israel, "If it seems good to you, and if it is of the LORD our God, let us send out to our brethren everywhere who are left in all the land of Israel, and

with them to the priests and Levites...and let us bring the ark of our God back to us, for we have not inquired at it since the days of Saul."

—1 Chronicles 13:1-3

In transporting the ark, David, according to God's divine instructions, surrounded it with two hundred eighty-eight singers and four thousand musicians to usher it into Jerusalem. When the priests took their God-ordained positions, the ark was transported into Jerusalem with great joy.

Moses placed a thick veil or curtain to protect the people from being killed by gazing at the *Shekinah* glory of God that rested upon the ark in the holy of holies. However, David did something so different that it is amazing. He placed singers and musicians full time before the ark. There was no veil to keep them from seeing God's glory. They saw the glory of God resting on the ark as they worshiped twenty-four hours a day.

David's Tabernacle in the End Times

A great restoration of God's power and presence will cover the earth in the End Times. The people of God will enjoy the divine presence, beauty and power of God in a way never before imagined. The glory of God will cover the earth as the waters cover the seas. And when the glory is manifested, the nations will look up to Jesus Christ, and multitudes upon multitudes will be saved in the greatest ingathering of souls in the history of mankind.

But Scripture holds some exciting keys as to how this incredible event will take place. It will not be according to a person's wonderful idea or program. But as lively stones, the members of the body of Christ will take their places within

193

the church and perform their many functions. God will help them, and the glory will be released in an awesome, final End-Time display.

What is most exciting is the role of worship and intercession. The priests got together not to preach or teach. They carried the ark of God's wonderful presence through divinely orchestrated and motivated worship.

David surrounded the ark with two hundred eighty-eight singers and four thousand musicians to minister to God. This resulted in the enemies of God being defeated. I believe this is a picture of the body of Christ functioning as living stones of the temple, surrounding the mighty presence of God and being vessels that release the anointing from heaven to earth in an incredible display of glory.

And although it's in mere seed form, I believe that twenty-four-hour prayer ministry around the world will play a part of this magnificent End-Time spectacle.

THE HARP AND BOWL

Now when He [Jesus] had taken the scroll, the four living creatures and the twenty-four elders fell down before the Lamb, each having a harp, and golden bowls full of incense, which are the prayers of the saints.

—REVELATION 5:8

The harp speaks of worship that includes God's music, and the bowl represents intercession. These two elements of worship rise up before the Lord in an interactive relationship of music and intercession performed by the king/priests as they are used to release God's presence on earth.

In Kansas City, we are at the very beginning stages of

developing what we refer to as the "harp and bowl" model of intercessory worship. We use this passage in Revelation as the foundation of our model of spiritual warfare. The harp and bowl speak of intercessory spiritual warfare operating with interaction between worship, music and prayers. As I have stated in earlier chapters, we are only at the beginning of our journey, and ten years from now things will be much more developed and sophisticated.

Like David, we are seeking God to discover how to express on the earth the worship that is in heaven. Jesus said to pray to see God's will on earth as it is in heaven. (See Matthew 6:10.) We want to see worship on earth as it is in heaven. I believe that God's fullness in worship comes first, and then the fullness of apostolic power comes second. Right now, we need to seek to operate in both of these.

We must seek to be extravagant worshipers as well as to be anointed servants of God fulfilling the Great Commission. I believe that the more we worship, the more we will fulfill the Great Commission with apostolic power from heaven.

There are many reasons why God has sovereignly established a harp and bowls around His throne. The harp, for example, is for music because at the core of God's being, He is a musician. The Holy Spirit is a musical Spirit, and the human spirit was created as a musical spirit, as well.

Truth is powerful and often moves our hearts deeply. God's truth combined with God's music opens the deepest places of our emotions, even at a level that truth without anointed music does not. God's truth blended with anointed music does several things. It touches us more deeply and brings us into greater unity in that it provides opportunity for many people in a room to experience the same depth of truth all at the same time.

In Psalm 133, it is evident that the commanded blessing will come when the saints enter into a supernatural unity.

> Behold, how good and how pleasant it is
> For brethren to dwell together in unity!
> It is like the precious oil upon the head,
> Running down on the beard,
> The beard of Aaron,
> Running down on the edge of his garments.
> It is like the dew of Hermon,
> Descending upon the mountains of Zion;
> For there the Lord commanded the blessing—
> Life forevermore.

God's truth with God's music unifies us in a profound way. Together we feel the same thing in the same moment, which is one component that God uses to unify us in the Spirit of God.

Hebrews 2:11-12 says that the Lord will release His songs and will sing them in the congregation.

> For both He who sanctifies and those who are being sanctified are all of one, for which reason He is not ashamed to call them brethren, saying: "I will declare Your name to My brethren; in the midst of the assembly I will sing praise to You."
>
> —HEBREWS 2:11-12

The Lord will give His songs to the people by the Spirit. In the midst of the assembly of the people of God, He will give His brethren the songs of the Lamb before the Father, and the songs of the Father before the Lamb!

Not only does the Son sing, but the Father also sings.

The LORD your God in your midst, the Mighty One, will save; He will rejoice over you with gladness, He will quiet you with His love, He will rejoice over you with singing.
                                                    —ZEPHANIAH 3:17

The Father and the Son are both singers, and the Holy Spirit is also a phenomenal musician. Together, they impart their music on the earth through the church. This music and these songs change the spiritual atmosphere of the cities in which they are released. As we pray and intercede together, we touch that beauty realm a little bit in our spirits when we function in the spirit and principles seen in the tabernacle of David.

DAVID'S MODEL OF INTERCESSION

THE KEY TO David's model of intercession was that he mixed three things together. David had two hundred eighty-eight singers and four thousand musicians taking shifts to minister to God before the ark for twenty-four hours each day. But the key factor was the prophetic spirit that came on the singers and musicians. This element of prophecy can be seen in 1 Chronicles 25.

Moreover David and the captains of the army separated for the service some of the sons of Asaph, of Heman, and of Jeduthun, who should prophesy with harps, stringed instruments, and cymbals.
                                                    —1 CHRONICLES 25:1

I am not using the word *prophetic* here in the sense of foretelling what is to come, although we can see in the Psalms that such prophetic foretelling was occasionally released in the midst of the people who were ministering in the tabernacle of

197

David. By prophetic spirit, I am referring to a spirit of inspiration from God. The atmosphere of heaven was imparted on them and through them. When the atmosphere of heaven is imparted on the singers and the musicians, the intercessors simply explode in the revelation of God's heart. We know that David joined the intercessors with the musicians and singers because a number of the Psalms were intercessory psalms written on site.

Admittedly, in Kansas City our rendition of the model of the prayer and worship in the spirit of the tabernacle of David is very weak and embryonic, but we are in a learning mode all the time. We desire to take the singers, the musicians and the intercessors and have them flow in what we call the harp and bowl model in this interactive relationship with one another.

Ezra was a leader who reestablished the Davidic order of worship in his generation. Nehemiah 11–12 presents a graphic and detailed description of the responsive, or the antiphonal, singing and speaking that occurred before the Lord.

Ezra 3:11 describes the activities of the responsive singer. One singer would sing, and the other would answer. One person would intercede for a moment, and then the singers would sing the prayer. The pattern would then be repeated.

> And they sang responsively, praising and giving thanks to the Lord: "For He is good, for His mercy endures forever toward Israel." Then all the people shouted with a great shout, when they praised the Lord, because the foundation of the house of the Lord was laid.

In our prayer ministry we use the apostolic prayers as our main New Testament model. For example, the flow may be something this: The drummer plays, and then the electric guitar plays; the singing starts, and then we pray. We pray Ephesians 1:17 for the Spirit of wisdom and revelation for the city. We pray 2 Thessalonians 3:1 for the city, that the Word of God would spread rapidly and that Jesus Christ would be glorified and direct us in the love of God across the city.

> That the God of our Lord Jesus Christ, the Father of glory, may give to you the spirit of wisdom and revelation in the knowledge of Him.
>
> —EPHESIANS 1:17

> Finally, brethren, pray for us, that the word of the Lord may run swiftly and be glorified, just as it is with you.
>
> —2 THESSALONIANS 3:1

These are some of the prayers that we pray, which were written by the apostles for the churches. These scriptures are used for training in the apostolic prayers, in other words, the prayers used by the New Testament apostles.

The second type of Scripture that we commonly use is found in the seventeen hymns of Revelation. We also use the Davidic psalms as a supplement and complement to the hymns of Revelation. We are using the language of these to touch the beauty realm. We sing through the Song of Solomon as well as the songs of the Old Testament prophets.

The working together of the singers, the musicians and the intercessors in the apostolic prayers, the hymns of Revelation, the Davidic psalms and the prophetic spirit results in the promise given in Isaiah:

> Even them I will bring to My holy mountain, and make them joyful in My house of prayer. Their burnt offerings

199

and their sacrifices will be accepted on My altar; for My house shall be called a house of prayer for all nations.

—ISAIAH 56:7

Jesus also quoted this verse when He entered Jerusalem and declared His kingdom. (See Matthew 21:13.)

In addition to the prayers we pray and sing, we envision developing antiphonal singing at the International House of Prayer. In ancient time, antiphonal choirs, with singers who answered one another back and forth in choruses and refrains, performed the songs of David. Antiphonal singing is also found in heaven.

The hymns of Revelation are antiphonal in style. For example, the church will sing, and then the angels respond, and then the twenty-four elders respond again. (See Revelation 5:8–14.) Notice that the singers and speakers within this particular celebration move five different times within seven verses. They are responding to one another in worship and intercession around the throne. This style is used around the throne throughout the Book of Revelation.

We desire to implement antiphonal singing in our intercessory ministry, but it is only in the planning phase right now because it takes skill and training to develop antiphonal choirs.

THE ATMOSPHERE OF THE HOUSE OF PRAYER

FORERUNNERS ARE NOURISHED and nurtured in the House of Prayer atmosphere. King David discusses this truth in Psalm 27:4 when he says that what he most wants to do is gaze at the beauty of the Lord. Once we've encountered such fascinating beauty, who would not want to gaze upon it continually? David inquires of the Lord as a prophet, and then he goes out to conquer the enemies of God as a king. After battle, David then returns as a priest and is cleansed, healed and washed.

So David first inquired of the Lord to receive divine strategy for God's purpose in any given season. In other words, he then became an apostolic emissary to defeat the enemies of God.

The tabernacle of David is vital in the process of gazing at the Lord, being empowered and being healed.

These battles are won outside of the prayer room in the natural after they are won first in the spirit in the House of Prayer. It is both a launching pad to go forth after having received divine strategy, and it is a place where battles are actually won in the realm of the spirit. The illustration in David's life shows us that this experience in prayer in his tabernacle was both a launching pad to action and a place of spiritual warfare to secure victory before the action.

As we train our intercessors and worshipers in Kansas City, we address participating in the heavenly symphony and the beauty realm of God. In all of creation, this spiritual place is the ultimate pinnacle of life and power. This place touches our emotions so that we feel and experience more power touching this realm than in any other place. This place in the heavenly symphony and beauty realm of God has commonly been overlooked by the body of Christ, but that is about to change. The Holy Spirit is going to get the attention of the body of Christ and focus it on this realm of God's beauty.

I only know a little bit about a few of the implications of this realm, but even what I do know is truly powerful. I'm just beginning to understand what it means to touch this realm of the Spirit. When we are in this realm, we are fascinated and exhilarated, and we become lovesick.

The fascinating God wants to cause the people of God on earth, as well as in heaven, to live in fascination with God.

Because we cannot endure much, the Lord God only allows little bits of that fascination to touch us. Our capacity is so limited that just a little bit goes a long way.

When we worship, life is at its best, and at the height of our worship, we stand upon that sea of glass gazing at His glorious throne. Worship sweeps us before God, allowing us to experience God's throne while we are still here on the earth. At the resurrection we will experience glory and participate in a far greater degree, but we need not wait for the resurrection. We must enter into it now. For the more we focus on it and the more we meditate on it, the more real it becomes.

As we seek the Lord to give us the pattern to reestablish the prayer ministry in the spirit of the tabernacle of David as a place for gazing upon His beauty and a place of refreshing and protection, we pray for a release of His anointing to do so. We ask Him to release the keys of David to unlock the tabernacle of David in this generation. We ask Him to cause lovers of Jesus Christ like yourself to come forth with hearts like David's, yearning to gaze upon His beautiful face.

And at midnight a cry was heard: "Behold, the bridegroom is coming; go out to meet him!"

—Matthew 25:6

12

JESUS
AS THE BRIDEGROOM,
KING AND JUDGE

I N THIS PRESENT hour, the Holy Spirit is emphasizing three
specific faces of Jesus: the Bridegroom, the King and the
Judge. It is clear to me that I cannot faithfully proclaim the
Bridegroom God if I do not present this message in full revelation of Jesus Christ as the Bridegroom, the King and the
Judge. Jesus Christ desires that we love all of who He is—not
just part of Him. We cannot be preachers of the Bridegroom
unless we prepare the way in judgment.

I have been considering how John the Baptist prepared
the way not only by preaching on the gladness of the
Bridegroom, but also by preaching on God's temporal and
eternal judgment, too. So also we cannot be preachers of
God's judgment unless we prepare the way in love by
declaring Him as the affectionate Bridegroom.

Jesus is called the King of kings for He has always existed
as King. (See Revelation 19:16.) He is King from eternity past
to eternity future. Jesus the great King with all power has the

heart of the Bridegroom. From eternity Jesus has burned with desire for us as the Bridegroom. As the King, He possesses all power, and as the Judge, He has the justice and zeal to remove all that hinders love.

So in this particular hour in history, I believe we will see the Holy Spirit's revelation of Jesus at a new height—and we find ourselves in an awesome, long-awaited moment in the unfolding mystery of the God.

A REVELATION OF JESUS CHRIST

FOR TWO THOUSAND years of church history the church has nearly neglected the revelation of Jesus as a Bridegroom. The subject of His burning desire for human beings has not been at center stage. Nevertheless, the Word of God contains prophecies clearly stating that the Messiah will be understood as a Bridegroom *before* He returns—not just afterward. Right now, the Holy Spirit is unlocking this understanding to the church throughout the world. You may very well be one of those being prepared to preach Jesus as the passionate Bridegroom.

We must remember that He is not only a Bridegroom, but He is also a King. He is a transcendent King who has power over the oceans, the sun, stars and the natural body. What He did in Exodus and Acts will be done once again. He will gather the peoples of the earth together in a great harvest in His role as King.

We have a limited understanding of Jesus as King. In fact, many of our worship songs declare His position as King, but we have little revelation of the Jesus who makes stars and whose word the oceans obey. We have yet to see the King heal thousands of paralytics with one word. Yet the Bible declares that in the End-Times He will move in the heavens, the stars, the weather, the oceans and the nations. He will demonstrate His kingly power by shaking everything that can be shaken.

> Therefore I will shake the heavens,
> And the earth will move out of her place,
> In the wrath of the LORD of hosts
> And in the day of His fierce anger.
>
> —ISAIAH 13:13

He is a transcendent King. I like to refer to our Savior as the "Jesus of Genesis 1"—in other words, as the Jesus who, being Himself the uncreated God, spoke to cause creation itself to spring forth from nothing. Recently, I have been studying Genesis 1 from a new perspective as a worshiper and as a lover of God. Phrase by phrase, passage by passage, I have exclaimed aloud, "Jesus, did You really do that?"

Jesus is the same Creator God now that He was in Genesis. This transcendent King is about to do great things on the stage of natural history before His Second Coming. Jesus Christ will be revealed in His transcendent power. He will stand up and be known in the earth.

> When You lift Yourself up, the nations shall be scattered; . . . "Now I will rise," says the LORD; "Now I will be exalted, now I will lift Myself up. . . . And the people shall be like the burnings of lime; . . . The sinners in Zion are afraid; fearfulness has seized the hypocrites: "Who among us shall dwell with the devouring fire?" . . . Your eyes will see the King in His beauty; . . . Your heart will meditate on terror: . . . But there the majestic LORD will be for us a place of broad rivers and streams . . . (For the LORD is our

207

> Judge, the LORD is our Lawgiver, the LORD is our King; He
> will save us); . . . And the inhabitant will not say, "I am sick";
> the people who dwell in it will be forgiven their iniquity.
> —ISAIAH 33:3, 10, 12, 14, 17–18, 21–22, 24

This mighty revelation of Christ's power will manifest His terrifying judgments. In addition, a greater dimension of healing miracles will be followed by unprecedented numbers of people being saved during the End Times.

I personally believe that God will end natural history in a display of the power like unto the power He used to begin it. In 2 Thessalonians, the apostle Paul describes the scene of the last day of natural history.

> When the Lord Jesus is revealed from heaven with His
> mighty angels, in flaming fire taking vengeance on those
> who do not know God, and on those who do not obey
> the gospel of our Lord Jesus Christ. These shall be pun-
> ished with everlasting destruction from the presence of
> the Lord and from the glory of His power, when He
> comes, in that Day, to be glorified in His saints and to be
> admired among all those who believe.
> —2 THESSALONIANS 1:7–10

When the curtain of time closes, Jesus will be in the clouds, with the entire sky filled with flaming fire, every angel of heaven circled to watch and all of the redeemed gathered together with Him. As heaven watches from the midst of this spectacle, the kings of the earth will run to the mountains asking them to crush them.

> He [Jesus] opened the sixth seal, and behold, there was a
> great earthquake; and the sun became black as sackcloth

208

of hair, and the moon became like blood. And the stars of heaven fell to the earth, as a fig tree drops its late figs when it is shaken by a mighty wind. Then the sky receded as a scroll when it is rolled up, and every mountain and island was moved out of its place. And the kings of the earth, the great men, the rich men, the commanders, the mighty men, every slave and every free man, hid themselves in the caves and in the rocks of the mounts, and said to the mountains and rocks, "Fall on us and hide us from the face of Him who sits on the throne and from the wrath of the Lamb! For the great day of His wrath has come, and who is able to stand?"

—REVELATION 6:12–17

Such an awesome hour of fury and glory will be comparable to the display of power that He manifested in Genesis 1.

What a powerful moment that will be! The Lover-Bridegroom, Gentle Shepherd and Lord of the Harvest is also coming as a righteous Judge. Before natural history is over, God will release His judgments upon the earth. These judgments will actually release His mercy and will increase the number of people receiving His redemption. For the Word of God says:

For when Your judgments are in the earth, the inhabitants of the world will learn righteousness.

—ISAIAH 26:9

The church in the Western world really has very little revelation or expectation of the Bridegroom God breaking into natural history as a terrifying judge. God's judgments are real, but from Genesis to Revelation they are stated clearly, time and time again.

God is even now raising up forerunners who will preach

the Bridegroom King as the Judge of all the living. This fore-runner ministry will instruct the church regarding God's purpose in releasing these inevitable judgments. It's important that the bride gain understanding of why the Bridegroom God must release His judgments. Without an understanding of how His judgments remove the things that hinder love, the very church Jesus loves could be tempted to draw back from Him by accusing Him of cruelty and harshness related to His judgments. Because God desires willing partnership from His church, she must understand that His judgments actually increase love in the earth, not destroy it. For us to have voluntary partnership we must have understanding and revelation. Anointed prophetic forerunners will prepare the way for the bride by proclaiming some of the wisdom and understanding that she must have to become ready to triumph in the days ahead. As events unfold, the mystery of God will be revealed.

Three main unprecedented activities will take place in the final generation. Although we looked at these in earlier chapters, I want to sum them up here.

THE FIRST COMMANDMENT
WILL BE RESTORED TO FIRST PLACE

FIRST OF ALL, God will restore the first commandment to first place. The people of God will love the Lord with all of their hearts. Passionate and extravagant lovers of God will become the norm in the church worldwide. The weak and broken in the church will be supernaturally empowered to love God with all of their hearts. This restoration will not be limited to special people or apostles, but will include housewives, businessmen and teenagers.

I want to prophesy to you by saying that the first commandment will be restored to first place in America before the Lord returns.

THE GREAT HARVEST

NEXT, THERE WILL be a great harvest of souls brought into the kingdom. More people will be saved than ever before in history. The power of God will be released, and God will bring the nations to His side. Just think about how many individuals are in the United States alone!

We do not really know what the great harvest will look like, but the Scriptures indicate that when the King shows His power, the multitudes will come in a very short amount of time. This appears to be happening already in some Third World countries. The numbers that are coming to the Lord in China, South America and Korea stretch our imaginations. Crusades of previously unimaginable sizes are becoming commonplace. The number of souls being harvested for the Lord keeps building and growing and growing. I may be wrong, but I believe we are in the beginning of the beginning of the last generation right now.

Some may say the Lord could come tonight. He might. I hope He does! However, I do not believe that He will; I believe that we still have some time before the Lord's return. I am not sure about when this will happen, but I believe it's not far away. It could happen within the next several decades.

UNPRECEDENTED TEMPORAL JUDGMENTS

REVELATION 9:15 MAKES a staggering statement; in fact, it is stated twice. It says that one-third of the entire earth will be killed by God's temporal judgments. One-third of the earth, one-third of the human beings on this planet will die related to catastrophic events in the final events before the Lord's return. Before the Second Coming of Christ, one-third of all the human beings on the earth will lose their lives in plagues as divine judgments are released.

> So the four angels, who had been prepared for the hour and day and month and year, were released to kill a third of mankind.
>
> —REVELATION 9:15

God's End-Time judgments have already begun. Earthquakes, plagues, chemical warfare and violence have increased at an alarming rate. If we listen carefully, we can hear the whisper before the shout.

IN CONCLUSION

THREE FACES OF Jesus Christ—Bridegroom, King and Judge— will be revealed and emphasized in the unprecedented End-Time activities of the Holy Spirit. These three faces can be seen in the restoration of the first commandment to first place, the great harvest and the release of the temporal judgments.

The revelation of the Bridegroom is what God will use to restore the first commandment to first place. Seeing the passionate Lover will make us passionate lovers of God. The revelation of the King will cause us to operate in the power of God as we go out to meet the great harvest. The revelation of the Judge will cause us to participate with Him in loosing His judgments.

As I end this book, I have only just begun. From here, I send you out to search. I encourage you to search the Scriptures and meditate on the Word of God. Open up your heart to the passionate Lover who is exhilarated and thrilled about you even while you are maturing in Him. Remember that God likes you and that you fill His heart with delight.

As you reach your heart toward Him, be encouraged that a powerful new dimension of His presence is waiting to unfold; it is the mystery of eternal ages, the heavenly Bridegroom and you—His beloved. The explosive power of this revelation will change you and make you ready to meet the challenges of holiness, compassion and beauty that await you in the glorious age in which you live. Your life is special. You have been prepared for such a time as this. You have been born for a purpose, and most important of all—

The best is yet to come!

NOTES

CHAPTER 7
THE PLEASURE OF HOLINESS

1. C. S. Lewis, *The Weight of Glory and Other Addresses* (Grand Rapids, MI: Eerdmans, 1965), 2.
2. John Piper, *Future Grace* (Sisters, OR: Multnomah, 1995), 9.
3. Sam Storms, *Pleasures Evermore: The Life-Changing Power of Enjoying God* (Colorado Springs, CO: NavPress, 2000), 31–32.

MINISTRY INFORMATION AND RESOURCES

Friends of the Bridegroom

Friends of the Bridegroom, led by Mike Bickle, provides ministry resources that help proclaim the forerunner message, equipping the church to live in her bridal identity with wholehearted love for Jesus in His threefold revelation as Bridegroom, King and Judge. The forerunner message proclaims three emphases of the Holy Spirit: (1) restoring the first commandment to first place; (2) an unprecedented demonstration of power resulting in the great harvest; and (3) a global release of the temporal judgments of God. For more information, visit our website at www.fotb.com.

Tabernacle of David Internship Program

This one-year resident training program in Kansas City, designed for singers and musicians between the ages of 18 and 25, focuses on training in the "harp and bowl" model of intercessory worship and prophetic music. Beginning in September each year, this program provides practical experience in leading worship and development of ministry skills. More information is available at www.fotb.com.

The Forerunner School of Prayer

This formal full-time training program will equip forerunners in several dimensions of prayer as well as training them with in-depth biblical studies to proclaim Jesus as Bridegroom, King and Judge. Our purpose is to equip them to function effectively in the Great Commission, and our primary objective is to see them fulfill the first commandment in their private lives. More information is available at www.fotb.com.

Friends of the Bridegroom Annual Conference

Held in either May or June, this conference helps to equip those who are called to the forerunner ministry. In addition to the teaching on subjects specifically related to the forerunner ministry, there is impartation, which releases new dimensions of revelation. For more details, visit our website at www.fotb.com.

International House of Prayer
Harp and Bowl Spiritual Warfare Conference

Held annually in October, this conference seeks to equip believers in the "harp and bowl" model of intercessory worship that is used in the International House of Prayer in Kansas City. Teaching sessions focus on practical application of the theology, principles and ministry skills necessary for this model. For more information, visit our website at www.ihopkc.com.

Harp and Bowl Intercessory
Worship Resources

Mike Bickle has developed many teaching resources to equip singers, musicians and intercessors to operate in the harp and bowl model of intercessory worship, flowing in a prophetic anointing in an interactive way. To order, call 1-800-552-2449, or visit our website at www.fotb.com.

Friends of the Bridegroom
Forerunner Ministry Resources

Resources are available to equip forerunners to proclaim the threefold revelation of the beauty of Jesus as Bridegroom, King and Judge. To order, call 1-800-552-2449, or visit our website at www.fotb.com.

Other Books by Mike Bickle

- *Passion for Jesus*
- *Growing in the Prophetic*

These books are available from your local Christian bookstore, or they can be ordered from Creation House by visiting our website at www.creationhouse.com.

FREE NEWSLETTERS
TO HELP EMPOWER YOUR LIFE

Why subscribe today?

- ❑ **DELIVERED DIRECTLY TO YOU.** All you have to do is open your inbox and read.

- ❑ **EXCLUSIVE CONTENT.** We cover the news overlooked by the mainstream press.

- ❑ **STAY CURRENT.** Find the latest court rulings, revivals, and cultural trends.

- ❑ **UPDATE OTHERS.** Easy to forward to friends and family with the click of your mouse.

CHOOSE THE E-NEWSLETTER THAT INTERESTS YOU MOST:

- • Christian news
- • Daily devotionals
- • Spiritual empowerment
- • And much, much more

SIGN UP AT: **http://freenewsletters.charismamag.com**

8178